Alison McNicol

The Craft BUSINESS Handbook

The Essential Guide
to Making Money
from your Crafts
and Handmade

A Kyle Craig Publication

www.kyle-craig.com

First published in 2012 by Kyle Craig Publishing

Text and illustration copyright © Alison McNicol

Design and illustration: Julie Anson

ISBN 978-1-908707-01-7

Contents

Chapter 7: *Signed, Sealed Delivered*

Chapter 8: *Show Me the Money!*

Chapter 9: *Onwards And Upwards!*

Craft Business Heroes: *Interviews*

Introduction

Introduction

If you're reading this book, chances are you've already spent more hours than you'd care to admit day-dreaming, fantasizing, about the fun, balanced, creatively fulfilling dream life you could be leading as a crafty entrepreneur! Master of your own destiny, captain of your own creative ship!

Maybe you have a great idea for a cool new line of products...or you're a designer but not quite sure how to turn those skills into a tangible business...or you're already making handmade items for friends, and want to up the ante and turn this into a profitable business...if only you could give up the day job and have the time and freedom to launch your own business, right?

These days it's easier than ever to become your own boss. And with the renewed popularity of traditional skills and handmade products, and consumers keener than ever to buying lovingly made unique items instead of mass-produced imported stuff, this really is the perfect time to get your creative business started. Plus, there are now so many tools out there to help you get a small business off the ground—you don't even need your own website to start selling goods online!

There is nothing more exciting than someone handing over their hard earned cash for something you have made...or visiting a store to see YOUR products on the shelves next to those of big, established brands. It's the biggest buzz there is!

Whether your goal is modest—to earn a little extra income and have fun selling a few items in your spare time. Or far more ambitious—to turn your creative ideas into a full-on, full-time business and see your product stocked in major stores world-wide—then this is the book for you!

Together we will look at the key steps to consider when planning your new business and new life!

Are you cut out for running your own business? What are your goals? How will you find the time, where will you work from? What will you make, who will you sell it to? Will you launch your own online store right away, or start with something like an Etsy store? Will you sell direct to the public at craft fairs, or only work from home selling online? If you're dreaming big, how will you grow your business, develop your brand, gain valuable PR, sell into stores? There is SO much to consider! We'll even look at some of the big dreams of many crafty entrepreneurs—getting press exposure, employing staff, getting stocked in major national stores, book deals and more!

With plenty of passion, planning, organisation, hard work and determination, your creative dreams really could come true…are you ready to take the next step?

My Story

Not so long ago, I had a very different career. As a PR executive in the music industry, I travelled the world, handling the publicity for some of the biggest music artists and bands around. It was my dream job, and one I had worked my socks off for. It was fun, glamorous, exciting…and incredibly hard work and long hours. Evenings were spent at gig after gig, late into the night, either in some hot, sticky underground dive bar or a massive, crowded stadium. Weekends were often more of the same, or travelling to and from interviews or photo-shoots. My time was not my own, and a personal life always came second to the job. After 15 years in the job (10 at major record labels, and 5 running my own successful PR company), I yearned for a simpler way of life. I dreamed of turning my childhood passion for 'making things' into some sort of business. A business that would allow me to work from home, be more involved in my own community, use my creative talents, and have that all-important work/life balance.

One day, after a particularly difficult meeting with a client, I decided that it was time for a change. Within weeks I had closed down my PR company, and with enough savings to last me 6 months, decided it was time for my new 'creative journey' to begin.

And what a journey that has been!

First up, I had the idea to teach kids sewing classes—I had been taught sewing at school from an early age, and as a child had loved to spend hours at my old vintage Singer machine (a Xmas gift when I was just 8) making outfits for my dollies, and gifts for friends and family. But I had noticed that these days it had all but disappeared from the school curriculum, and so many children I knew had no idea how to sew or even thread a needle—how sad that a whole generation of kids would miss out on the simple pleasures of being able to sew.

I felt the time was right and that traditional skills were ready to make a comeback. My hunch was so right. It was 2005, and within a few years the whole sewing and knitting revival was in full swing.

Right from the beginning, I knew I wanted this to be a real business, not just me in the local church hall teaching a couple of days a week. I was thinking BIG! I trademarked my Stitchclub brand, spent a fortune on a flashy website, and within 12 months I had a team of teachers running Stitchclub classes in 30 locations across the country. Less than a year later I had franchised the brand nationally and was preparing to expand internationally. Things were going great. And then the dreaded "recession" kicked in...more of that later...

As the Stitchclub brand grew, the next logical step was to create a line of products—in my case a range of kids and adults sewing and craft kits. That way I could reach all the potential customers out there, who by now were e-mailing from not just all over the country, but all over the world. The demand for classes was exceeding the speed at which the franchise operation was adding new teachers and locations, and it was frustrating to be turning away potential customers with a "sorry we don't have a class near you yet", so this seemed like a great way to turn all the interest and attention into some sort of revenue.

Launching a product line! Now what a learning curve that was!!! From sourcing parts, designing and printing packaging, production, manufacturing, trade shows, selling to major retailers, dealing with barcodes, health & safety, employing staff, order fulfillment...there was so much to learn. Within months of launching at a major trade show, I secured orders from the biggest chain of department stores in the country! A huge coup, or so I thought at the time...a whirlwind 6 months later the kits were on the shelves in time for Xmas.

Thanks to my PR skills I gained tons of press coverage in glossy magazines and newspapers, and soon had my own magazine column in a leading craft magazine. Next came a TV appearance, a book deal, and sponsorship from several major craft companies, one of whom provided free sewing machines to ALL my teachers to use in their classes. I was even approached by a TV production company, and we pitched a sewing show concept to one of the nation's biggest TV channels. Amazing, huh?

Now if all this sounds like the kind of stuff you dream about, then you're absolutely right. So many amazing things happened, and so much went right for me. I ticked more things off of my "business dream list" than even I could have imagined when I started out.

Then came the dreaded recession, sales plummeted and the bank called in my large business loan. I had simply borrowed too much to grow the business, and now I couldn't make the loan payments. I fought long and hard to save the business, but ultimately it ended in bankruptcy and losing my home. You can bet that definitely wasn't on the list! I bet big, and I lost big!

Stitched Up!!

So I must have done a lot of things right, to have achieved so many amazing business opportunities. But clearly there was plenty I did that wasn't so right. Closing down my profitable PR business before I had even launched Stitchclub probably wasn't the best idea, with hindsight. I was single, with a large mortgage to cover, and no one to share the financial burden with. Perhaps if I had been able to keep earning while I got things off the ground, I wouldn't have raced through my savings so quickly and started the debts and borrowing that would ultimately be me, and my company's, downfall. The way I financed my business and accrued so much debt right from the start meant that just at the point where things were really taking off—ironically business was going better than ever—the whole thing came tumbling down and I was forced to sell my home and pretty much declare myself bankrupt as I simply couldn't keep up with all the loan repayments. Quite simply, the debts were strangling the business, and without cashflow, it was impossible to grow the business to increase income. Without cashflow, no business can survive. I guess that's my only regret.

So, while I'm no business expert—and would never claim to be —in the past 5 years I've probably learned more, laughed more, cried more, and grown more, both as a person, and as a 'business person' than at any other time in my adult life. It's been a roller coaster full of highs—I'll never forget the buzz of seeing my very own products on sale in the country's biggest department stores!—to the lows—having to sell my beloved home and lose everything I worked so hard for.

But every single day, I felt alive. Alive and excited about what surprises that day would bring. When you're running your own business, no two days are the same, and the possibilities are endless!

Now I'm back on track and more driven than ever. I learned a lot about my strengths and weaknesses, as well as what I do and don't want from my career. I realized that what I love to do most is create, and communicate (you can take the girl out of PR...) And so now, I'm a writer. I feel that everything happens for a reason, and if all that I've been through has brought me to this place, then it was worth it. I've finally found my true calling, and I've never been happier.

I was inspired to write this book to share all that I've learned during this crazy ride, and to hopefully help others benefit from the amazing things I learned along the way, but also avoid the pitfalls so you don't end up like I did! I imagined the kind of practical and inspirational business book that I would have killed for 5 years ago—oh, there is SO much I wish I had known up-front! I wanted to share the business stuff that no one tells you about, plus I've also spoken with some of the most interesting creative entrepreneurs out there, who have been so generous with their time and advice, and I hope you enjoying reading about their experiences and insider tips as much as I have!

So—is starting your own crafty business right for you?

There's only one way to find out...let's get started!

Alison McNicol x

Chapter 1

I Craft, Therefore I am

Who are you? What do you dream of?

The fact that you're reading this book makes me think that you've probably already been thinking about this for a while, right? Have you spent hours, days, weeks, months even, daydreaming about your wonderful new creative business life? Imagining how happy and fulfilled you'll be—spending your days designing, creating, making, selling. Well now it's time to turn those dreams into reality!

Every one of us will have a completely different picture of how we would like our 'dream life' to be.

Perhaps you've imagined yourself wafting around your huge, white, light-filled studio, spending your days choosing fabric samples, tinkering around with bead combinations for your latest genius design, fielding calls from department stores and cool boutiques desperate to stock your creations, clipping press cuttings of yet another A-list celeb wearing/toting/raving about your latest collection...It's definitely only a matter of time before fame, riches and immeasurable success finds you, right?

Or you may be motivated purely by the artistic endeavour of creating something beautiful and putting it out there into the world, for all to enjoy. You just love to make things, and simply want to earn enough from your craft to pay for new craft supplies and make your hobby pay for itself.

Perhaps you're stuck in a 9 to 5 job that no longer challenges you, and just being able to make the same money doing what you love would be a dream come true. Or you may be a stay at home parent, desperate to do something for 'you' (and earn some much needed extra income while you're at it!).

It may even be that like I did, you have a much more commercial vision and dream of creating a brand—seeing your designs and products on the pages of magazines, and on the shelves of major stores and being stocked in the best stores internationally.

Whatever your dreams are, you absolutely have the power to make them happen. Now I can't promise you that you'll get exactly what you're dreaming of, or that things will go just as you expect them to, or that everything will turn out exactly as you planned! Because that would be SO boring and predictable! But I can say this for sure—taking the leap into working for yourself, and following your creative dreams, will be one of the most rewarding and empowering things you will ever do.

Now—there's just a few things to figure out before you get started. Are you ready?

It's good to have a very honest talk with yourself, at this early stage, to figure out what makes you tick. Try the checklist below, and circle what speaks to you. It's interesting to refer back to this as your business progresses.

What's My Motivation?

- I want to make a ton of money
- I want to work from home
- I want to see my products in BIG stores all over the country/world
- I want to create a brand
- I want to feel challenged
- I want to do something for ME
- I want the recognition, and to be known for my work
- I want to leave a job I hate
- I want to be able to create, every day
- I want to help charities
- I want to do something to help the environment
- I want to create local jobs
- Other _____
- Other _____

Time for some...visualization

Starting a business to sell your crafts isn't just about making stuff and selling it to people. The whole point is to create the most important thing in the world—your ideal life! Or working life at least! When you dream of starting your own creative business, no doubt you will be imagining the products you'll create and the people who will buy them...but without a doubt you will be imagining the LIFE you'll be leading as you do this!

The best thing about being your own boss it that YOU get to decide how your working life will be. Perhaps just the idea of being able to work alone, making your jewelry, in a studio at the end of the garden is your idea of bliss. Or travelling all over the country to craft and trade fairs and meeting thousands of interesting new people, and customers, floats your boat. The great thing is, YOU can decide what shape your life will take, and YOU have the power to make it all happen.

Close your eyes and try to visualize your new working life:

Imagine your ideal working day...

• What time will you start work at?

• Where will you work from?

• Who will be there?

• What will the day hold?

• What will you make?

• What other tasks will you do?

• How will you feel?

Now imagine how this can be improved upon as you work hard to grow your business. What will the picture look like in 2 years... in 5 years?

Take 5 mins to close your eyes and daydream about your new life... how it feels, how it looks, how it develops as your business grows...

Hold that picture in your mind...now it's time to start making your dreams a reality!

66 Choose a job you love, and you will never have to work a day in your life. 99
Confucius

What are your Expectations?

As well as imagining the look, feel and future of your potential new business, setting some clear goals right at the start helps keep you focused, and is a great way of motivating you and keeping you on track. Like anything in life, you'll get back what you put in—so if you're aiming high, then you need to be prepared to put in the hard work in order to reap the rewards.

Ask any creative business person and they will tell you that, in order to make enough income to live on, or to replace a regular job, you'll need to work harder than you ever have in your life. Are you willing to give up your evenings and weekends at first, and see less of your friends and family? Does the idea of eating, sleeping and breathing your business appeal to you? Are you willing to do whatever it takes to make your business a success? If the answer to any of these is no, then that's absolutely OK. Not everyone is aiming for world domination, or to be the next Martha Stewart! You have to figure out what is right for YOU!

Are you willing to leave your comfort zone?

Perhaps you're not a natural salesperson? If you're incredibly shy, chances are that the idea of blowing your own trumpet, selling directly to the public, presenting your range to a buyer from a retailer, or being interviewed by a craft magazine brings you out in a cold sweat. Are you willing to take a deep breath and overcome your fears?

Or perhaps you don't consider yourself a natural 'business' person. Many right-brain creative people are terrified at the idea of dealing with the paperwork involved in running a business. The thought of keeping accounts, filing tax returns and dealing with bureaucracy can be scary —but it's actually way easier than you may think and hey, that's what accountants are for!

Before you get started, have a serious think about what you ARE willing to do to achieve your business goals, what sacrifices you are willing to make, and what aspects of your life are simply non-negotiable. Doing so at this early stage is really helpful as once a new business begins, it can take over your life without you even realizing it! Do you think you have what it takes to succeed?

**Key Characteristics of a
Successful Entrepreneur**

Creative

Self-confident

Persistent

Competitive

Goal-oriented

Willing to take calculated risks

Take A few Moments to Consider Your Ideal Working Life:

- How many hours per day am I willing to work?
- How many hours a week can I spare RIGHT now?
- Am I willing to travel, or will I only work from home?
- Am I OK with working weekends if necessary?
- Am I willing to give up my social life at first?
- How much cash do I have to get started?
- Can I survive financially while the business grows?
- What are my monetary goals?
- Do I want this to be a full-time occupation?
- Will I be ok with making the same things every day, often in volume?
- How many items can I imagine making each week?
- Am I willing to employ others in order to grow the business?
- Will I enjoy dealing with the public?
- How soon am I able get started?
- What scares me about this?

Find some…Inspiration

Whether it's creating a new design or imagining the possibilities for a new business, we all need plenty of inspiration to really get those creative juices flowing. There's nothing like checking out the competition, or seeking out other creative artists and business people whose careers you admire (and perhaps envy!) to really give you a clear picture of the possibilities that are in store.

Personally, I absolutely love reading business books that contain interviews with real people. I love hearing about how they got started, the challenges they faced, and how they reached the success they have today. That's why one of my favorite parts of this book was interviewing all the amazing crafty entrepreneurs and gathering their stories to share with you. In fact, I got so carried away, that I've filled a second book, **'Craft Business Heroes'**, with even more inspirational people and their stories. It's by reading these true accounts of ordinary people achieving extraordinary things that we think "Hey, if they can do that, maybe I can too."

Who is your inspiration? Look around—what designers do you admire? Whose career do you envy? How did they get started? What are they doing now? Whether you're a fabric designer who dreams of being the next Amy Butler, or a potter dreaming of being the next Jonathan Adler, no matter what your creative niche, it's easy to find someone to admire and provide inspiration. Check out their website for a biog, Google them to find old magazine articles, find out their story. What do you love about their career? What do their products represent that you love?

For crafters out there, there has never been more opportunity to network and communicate with others. There are tons of amazing crafty blogs, e-zines, magazines and websites out there bringing together crafters and creatives from all over the world. Warning—it's easy to lose hours, days, of your life online in the name of 'research'!

Take a class, join a craft workshop or group locally, get to know the owner of your local crafty stores or galleries (chances are, if you're reading this book, you're probably already involved in many of these things, *thankyouverymuch*, so apologies if I'm stating the obvious here!)

Another fantastic way of seeing what the future could hold for you is by visiting local craft shows, gift shops and galleries. What products do you love, how have they laid out their stall or booth—"wow, check out their amazing logo and packaging...what a cool way to hang the necklaces..." And don't be afraid to chat to stallholders—every one of them was in your position once, and most will be more than happy to offer advice.

STOP the...Procrastination

I don't know about you, but I can quite happily while away hours, days, weeks, even months daydreaming. In fact, I'm so full of wonderful ideas, I reckon I could quite easily make a full time career out of visualizing and imagining all the wonderful things I could/would do...if only I had the time/tools/money/support etc!

Even when it came down to writing this book, something I was hugely excited about, and knew exactly what I wanted to say, and how I wanted to say it, it took me longer than planned as I simply kept putting off getting started! Sometimes the idea of something can be so overwhelming, the task seems so massive, that we find ourselves putting off getting started day after day.

It can often seem easier to find a millions reasons why you can't or shouldn't get started on an idea right away, but eventually, the desire to create wins through. And it's true what they say about baby steps/bite-sized chunks/one step at a time and all that. By breaking the task down into small achievable goals, and taking a deep breath and doing just one thing—suddenly you find yourself one step closer to your goal.

If you're still waiting for the 'right' time—it may never come. Will you ever have enough time/money/freedom/support/space/energy to fulfill your dreams? Maybe. Maybe not. Maybe you already have all of those things, but you just don't realize it. These days you really don't need thousands to start a small business. And even a few hours a week is enough to get going.

So—what's stopping you?

> *Twenty years from now you will be more disappointed by the things that you didn't do than by the ones you did do. So throw off the bowlines. Sail away from the safe harbor. Catch the trade winds in your sails. Explore. Dream. Discover.*
> *Mark Twain*

Prepare your...Situation

If you're currently working full-time, or your days are jam packed with childcare and family commitments, it can be hard to find the time, let alone the energy, to get started on a new project.

If you're going to find the time to really commit to your new business, you need to treat your 'craft business time' as an appointment that is just as important as any other. Just as you would a dentist appointment, or a meeting at your child's school, pencil your 'CBT' into your diary, even if it's just a 2-3 hour shift once a week to begin with.

If you have children, perhaps you could ask a friend or relative to baby-sit for the odd evening or afternoon to free you up. Or take a good, hard look at your week and how you spend your time—could you save those 3 hours spent travelling to and from the supermarket by ordering online? Or give book club a miss for a couple of months while you get started?

By making a conscious effort to schedule the time for your new venture, with each day that passes the task will feel less daunting—the more you do the more you will be inclined to do—and you'll be up and running before you know it!

Start With a Bang!

If at all possible, could you take
a week's 'creative vacation' from your job?
I'm sure you'd much rather spend a week
off work relaxing on a beach somewhere tropical,
but dedicating a chunk of time could
be just the boost you need to get started!

66 Take the first step in faith. You don't have to see the whole staircase, just take the first step. 99
Dr. Martin Luther King Jr.

It's all about...Communication

Talk to friends and family, tell them your plans. When you've spent months excitedly planning your new business, it can sometimes be quite daunting to share your hopes and dreams with others. What if they laugh? What if they react negatively and tell you you're crazy? What if they just don't get it?

Well that's ok. Each of us operate differently, and for some people out there, the idea of giving up a well-paid career, or risking time and money on a 'pipe-dream creative venture' may seem absolutely crazy.

If your mother, partner or best friend is perhaps not the most creative type, and would never in a million years understand how you could even think of trying to make a living following what you love, then perhaps they're not the best people to start with—you can tell them later, when you have really gotten things off the ground and can impress them with what you have already achieved!

There will always be people who won't quite understand what you're doing, and those who support you and can be relied upon to help out when the going gets tough.

Even the most negative feedback can be helpful—friends can troubleshoot and ask questions about your business plans that will highlight an area that perhaps you hadn't considered, and provide an objective eye.

Knowing that your friends and loved ones will be following your progress and asking how things are going on a regular basis can be a great motivator! In fact, I deliberately told plenty of people that I was writing this book, and when I aimed to have it finished by. At times it was sheer shame of admitting that I hadn't actually hit my targets that week that led me to sit my ass back in the chair and get another few thousand words done!

And by putting your plans 'out there', it can set off a whole chain of events...one friend may mention you to a colleague and before you know it, you have a fellow crafty entrepreneur to swap tips with, or a whole set of new ideas for your business you hadn't yet considered!

What's Your Plan?

So—are you clear on what you want to achieve now? What are your goals? How will your new life look?

My Aims....	In 6 months	In 2 years	In 5 years
Working hours per week			
Working during evenings and weekends?			
Make the following products			
Work from this location			
Have this many staff			
Have my products in this many stores			
Pay myself this per month			
Other			
Other			

Just Go For It!

No two days will be the same.
You'll find out your true strengths. And your weaknesses.
You will learn more about yourself in that first year of business, than in all the previous years of working put together.
You'll surprise yourself, and be proud of yourself, on a daily basis.
If you don't give it a try, you'll never know!

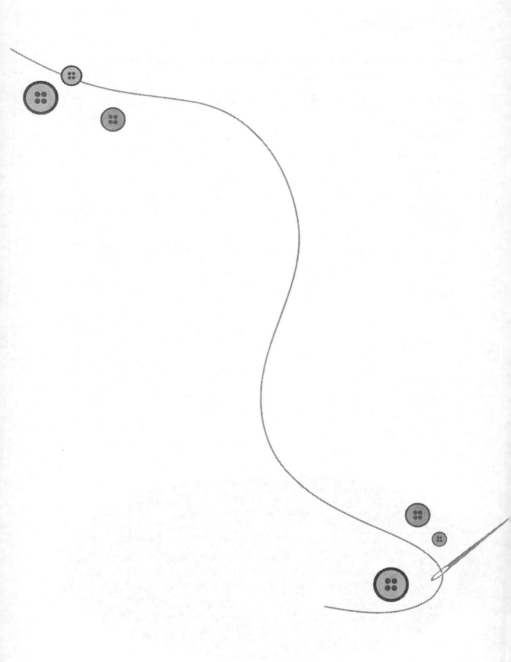

Chapter 2

A Brand New You

I'm With The Brand!

No matter how big or small your aims are for this new business, it's important to have a clear image of how you see your 'brand' right from the start. Nowadays, even small home-based businesses present themselves in highly professional, stylish and creative ways that could rival even the 'big boys'! You only have to look on the likes of Etsy to see thousands of crafty business people who have taken the time to create a unique visual identity for their small businesses—it really is the key to being taken seriously these days.

Now this doesn't mean that you have to spend thousands on expensive designers and brand experts—armed with a little knowledge you can easily create yourself a 'brand identity' all of your own. Whether you go for just a logo and a great URL to begin with, or you're planning big things and decide to Trademark and protect your intellectual property (more of this later), getting your 'brand' right is the first step to having a successful business.

Fake it 'Till You Make It!

You may currently be a one-man-band working flat out making your products in a tiny spare room above the garage, but present yourself and your company in the right way and customers could quite easily assume that they're dealing with an already highly successful company!

In the early days of my business, friends of mine used to laugh when they'd hear me refer to the company as 'we'! "Ah yes," I'd say, "we're busy launching a great new line of kits this autumn and we're really excited about their potential." In reality 'we' was myself, at the kitchen table, frantically making those very kits, boxing them, sending invoices, driving to trade shows, running the 'customer service department', doing absolutely everything myself! But I was thinking big, and with the time and effort I had spent on branding, logos, website and design, the company already looked like a 'proper business', so I simply wanted to act like it was already the success I knew it could and would be! There eventually was a 'we'—a great team came together as the company grew. But in the meantime, whether I was speaking to a buyer at a trade show, or discussing my company with a magazine journalist, what harm did it do to present my company and brand as a 'we'—so much more than just a 'me'!

Now I'm certainly not suggesting that you all lie and start misleading people about the true nature of your business, for there is absolutely nothing wrong with being a designer/maker building an exciting new company on your own, and often that can be a key part of your appeal. The message is that it pays to act as though you're already a success, right from the start. You'll send out the right message, come across as truly professional, and gain the respect and attention you and your products deserve!

Identify Yourself:
The Key Elements of a Great Brand

Image/Personality: What do you want your company to be known for? Fun? Innovation? Green credentials? Quality? Craftsmanship? Quirkiness?

Choose a Name: Don't let it pigeon hole you i.e. 'Cookie's Cards' or 'Bag-tastic'! Think about not only what you are making now, but what you could potentially make in the future. There's no point in having a name like 'Bag-tastic' and a logo shaped like a handbag when for all you know, your could end up making a range of shoes or slippers that become your leading products—in 5 years time you could be running a successful shoe company...called, er...'Bag-tastic'!

Mission Statement: Can you describe, in no more than 100 words, the essence and unique qualities of your brand/company? For example: 'Kidsville' is a company creating fun, natural children's toys and accessories, with a modern twist on traditional toy and nursery designs. From our recycled bottle top 'spinning tops' to our best-selling 'TinyTrike'—all products are made in the USA from 100% natural and recycled products.

Have a look at the keywords below and circle those that you feel best describe your ethos, your products, or your ideal brand image:

Keywords

Handmade   Innovative

Traditional   Green

Slick   Retro

Technology   Fun   Natural

Witty   Quirky   Quality

Craftsman

Honest   Ethical   Soft   Luxury

Earthy   Feminine   Recyclable

Sustainable

Youthful   Value for Money

Funky

Bohemian   Edgy   Glamorous

Durable

Healthy   Organic

Revolutionary

Practical

Clean   Time-saving   Gothic

Whimsical   Modern   Decadent

Happy   Sensuous

Inpisiring   Odd

Radical   Sexy   Fresh

Cooky

Masculine   Cute

Feminine

Tasty   Children

Indulgent   Fragranced   Vibrant

Other words to describe your product/ethos/image:

Now...time to brainstorm some ideas for names, and decide on your mission statement:

Company Name Ideas:

Mission Statement:

Check your Company Name

Before you set your heart on a company name and start spending money on website domains and logos, it's important to double check that someone else isn't already out there trading under the same name.

First up, check in the kind of areas you'll be trading in initially. Look on Etsy where you can 'search for a seller' and see if there are any other crafty businesses with a similar name to you. Do a Google search and see what comes up. If you're in luck so far, the next step is to check with all the relevant official agencies to see if anyone in your state, or nationally, is trading under that name.

At state/local level you should look up the website of your state Corporation Division. Most will offer online searches where you simply type in to search for a business name. You can find a list and links to each state website at:

www.secstates.com

All clear at state level? Check that no big national companies are trading under your name or similar by checking at the US Patents and Trademarks Office:

www.uspto.gov

Once you have checked thoroughly and have the all clear, you are ready to register your company name and should file what is known as a DBA (doing business as) registration with your county clerk.

In the UK , after you have searched online for websites of any very small businesses with your name or similar, to check if any businesses are actually registered, one search is all you need, at Companies House at

www.companieshouse.gov.uk

If you have BIG plans for world domination, it's worth checking your potential business name in all the major English-speaking countries —USA, UK, Canada, Australia and New Zealand!

My Company Name Is Going To Be:

Get a Domain Name

Your domain name, or URL, is the address of your website. If you decided to call your company 'Kidsville', then the perfect URL would be 'www.kidsville.com' You want it to be memorable, easy to type, and unlikely to result in spelling mistakes. For instance 'www.kidsville-recycled-toys.com' would be just too long and would allow for too many opportunities for customers to make an error when typing. There are thousands of companies who will help you search for and register a domain name. Some of these also offer hosting for websites, e-mail accounts, website building tools and even e-commerce solutions.

Registering your domain name is pretty cheap—it can be as little as $10 a year, and you retain ownership of that domain as long as you pay and renew. If you fail to renew and let it lapse even for a day, someone else could buy it. So it's worth paying for a couple of years up-front, enabling an 'auto-renew' feature for your bank account, and making sure your contact details on your account stay up to date so they can send you a renewal reminder. Here are just a few companies to check out:

USA

www.godaddy.com

www.register.com

www.namesecure.com

UK

www.ukwebsolutionsdirect.co.uk

www.godaddy.com/uk

So before you set your heart on your company name, you should do a web search to see if the best domain name is available. If your first choice domain is available, fantastic, register it quick, and also I'd recommend registering several variations—.com, .net, .co.uk and so on. This isn't that YOU will necessarily use them—though who knows when you may be ready to expand internationally! It will at least prevent someone else in another country launching a website that your customers may accidentally go to. Especially if they're selling a similar kind of product.

Now it may be that 'Kidsville.com' will come up as 'unavailable'. Either it has been bought by a company which makes a living from registering millions of domain names in the hope that people just like you will come along and offer to buy one from them, or someone is actually using it for their own business. Quite simply putting the web address into your search bar will reveal all. You will either find a very interesting company called 'Kidsville' running summer camps for kids, or you may find a web company asking you to 'make them an offer'!

This has happened to me in the past. Because I was at such an early stage of deciding on the company name, rather than risk paying hundreds or thousands for a URL I didn't absolutely need, I went back to the drawing board and came up with a new company name that I could find the right URL for.

So, deciding on your company name, and getting your Domain Name should really go hand-in-hand!

Belt and Braces!

Once you've finalized your company name and registered your main domain name, you may want to safeguard your brand even further.

Depending on your company/domain name, it's good to have a think about other spellings of your product or company name, or the same name with an 's' on the end and register those too. If you end up with a successful company, there will always be unscrupulous people who will buy a very similar domain, set up selling similar products, all with the intention of benefitting from YOUR brand and marketing power and picking up a % of your customers.

In the case of our imaginary company 'Kidsville', perhaps 'www.kidsville-toys.com' would be a good one to protect. Also maybe 'www.kidsvill.com' to allow for typing errors?

As and when you have some key products, you may also consider registering domains for those too. So while your company site may be 'Kidsville.com', you could also register 'www.tinytrike.com'. You can have several different domains 'point' to the same website—so while your main website may be 'Kidsville.com' you could have the Tiny Trike url point to it. Who knows—one day Tiny Trike may be such a huge brand of its own that it requires its very own website!

Domain Name Search

Available:

Not Available:

Domains I am going to register:

Logo

Pretty much every business you can think of has a logo. Your logo should tie in clearly with the image you want to project for your business. Your logo could be a picture, a graphic symbol, or even just a simple monogram using the key letters of your business name.

Think about your company mission statement and the keywords you feel best describe your business. If you see your business and products as fun, quirky, rebellious and alternative, then a bland two letter logo may not best represent you visually. Likewise, if you're producing, say, an organic skincare range and want to portray an image of purity, nature and luxury, then a cartoon goldfish probably isn't going to send out the right message to your customers either! You want a logo that will reflect your company's personality, products and mission statement, and appeal to the type of customer you feel would buy your products—all in one small image. Easy, right?!

Whenever I've been stumped for logo ideas, I have a good look around at other companies for inspiration. Who is my customer? Where else might he or she shop? What other sort of brands and products might they be attracted to? By looking at logos I loved, and those I wasn't so keen on, I began to form ideas for my own.

Who are your customers? What other brands would your typical customer buy? Have a look around and start noting and sketching any logos that you love, and think about how they represent that brand.

Inspiration is everywhere.

Perhaps you love the way one company uses a clean, simple line drawing to portray honesty and simplicity. Or how another cleverly uses the shapes of the letters of their name in combination with a picture of their key product. Think about how you could apply that general idea to your own logo.

It goes without saying that there's a big difference between being inspired by another person's logo or website design and out and out ripping it off, so be careful!

LOGO 101

Simple

Memorable

Communicates clearly the personality of your business

Works well in both Black & White and Color

Colors

Now you may have decided on a simple black on white line drawing for your logo, which is fine. But if you're going for a full color logo, then the colors you will use are just as important as the logo style itself.

Again, think about your products, your 'brand', and the colors that best represent your mission statement.

Cool Colors tend to have a calming effect. At one end of the spectrum they are cold, impersonal, antiseptic colors. At the other end the cool colors are comforting and nurturing. Blue, green, and the neutrals white, gray, and silver are examples of cool colors.

Warm colors convey emotions from simple optimism to strong violence. The warmth of red, yellow, pink, or orange can create excitement or even anger. The neutrals of black and brown also carry attributes of warm colors.

Metallics: While it may be tempting to opt for silver or gold—particularly if you are a jeweller, or wish to portray a luxurious brand image…but be aware that this will mean more expensive printing costs on all of your packaging, business cards, flyers etc. Special spot color processes for metallics can be very expensive, and you may soon live to regret your silver logo when it's time to print 5,000 boxes and the cost is double what it could be!

PMS Pantone Colors

No, PMS colors are not the color of chocolate or wine when you're feeling rather hormonal—PMS stands for Pantone Matching System! Pantones are a standardized ink color system used in the printing industry, to ensure that images and logos are created in exactly the same colors no matter where you choose to have your item printed. You may find that you use different printing companies for your flyers than for your packaging or stickers etc. So if your logo uses Pantone PMS 1915 (Pink) and PMS 9235 (blue), then you would quote that to every printer you work with to ensure continuity across all your printed matter.

Typeface/Font

The typeface you use for your logo and other business literature can communicate a lot about your image, so choose carefully. In addition to those already available on your computer there are plenty available for free download online. If you're using a designer to help with logos and flyers, they will probably already have a great selection to choose from.

Understanding the Use of Colors for Printing and Manufacturing

There are several types of printing processes—and often you may be asked to choose, which can be rather confusing! Worry not—there are two main printing processes you will need to know about: 4 color process (CMYK) printing and Spot Color Printing.

CMYK: also called 4 color process printing, involves the use of four plates: Cyan, Magenta, Yellow and Keyline (Black). The CMYK artwork (which you will have supplied) is separated into these four colors—one plate per color. The four CMYK inks are applied one by one to four different rollers and the paper or card ('stock') is then fed through the printing press. The colors are applied to the stock one by one, and out comes the full color (4 color process) result.

Spot Color Printing: Typically used for jobs which require no full color imagery, such as for business cards and other stationery, or in monotone (or duotone etc.) literature such as black and white newspaper print.

Spot color printing creates brighter, more vibrant results, but with a smaller color range. When printing in single (spot) colors, a single color ink (normally with a Pantone reference number) is applied to the printing press roller. If there is just one color to be printed, there will be a single plate, and a single run of the press. If there are two colors, there will be two plates and two runs, and so on. The colors are layered onto the paper one by one.

So Why Do I Need to Know This?
This means that the artwork you, or whoever is creating your logo produces, either has to be spot color artwork or CMYK artwork.

Colors and their meanings:

Cool Colors

Blue – water, fresh, strong, important, peaceful, intelligent

Turquoise – feminine, sophisticated, retro

Silver – sleek, glamorous, rich

Lavender – graceful, elegance, delicate, feminine

Warm Colors

Red – sexy, hot, love, passion, heat, joy, power

Orange – energy, warmth change, health

Pink – sweet, nice, romance, playful, delicate

Yellow – happy, joy, cheerful, remembrance

Green – organic, healthy, natural, growth, environment, harmony

Purple – royal, precious, romantic, sacred, hippy, gothic

Gold – riches, extravagance, traditional

Neutral colors

Beige – conservative, relaxing

White – clean, classic, purity, innocence, softness

Black – conservative, mysterious, sophisticated, gothic

Grey/Gray – formal, conservative, sophisticated

Ivory – quiet, pleasant, understated elegance

Brown – earthiness, wholesomeness, simplicity, friendliness

Your Logo Ideas

Have a think about what sort of logo would work best for you. What colors can you visualize? Will it contain a shape or image, or just text?

Colors:

Images or Shapes to use:

Sketch some logo ideas here:

Chapter 3

Mind Your
Own
Business!

Office Essentials

There are a few tools essential to running a good business—most of which you may already have—and you don't need to spend a fortune to get business-ready!

Set up your office area somewhere in the home away from distractions —you really don't want to be dealing with a journalist or speaking to a retailer about your products to the sound of the kids squabbling or cartoons in the background! Even if it's a nook under the stairs, a section of the basement or, if you're lucky enough, a dedicated office building/shed at the end of the garden, it's great to have an area that is all about business that you can close the door to at the end of the day.

For many people working from home, space may be limited, but if at all possible try to keep your creative space and your business space separate. It can be pretty hard to concentrate on a business plan or raising invoices when you're surrounded by pieces of fabric and piles of buttons! Perhaps your craft room/making room will be in a spare bedroom, and your office area in a corner of the dining room. Whatever works for you!

Dedicated Phone Line

It's never a good idea to use your home phone as a business line—just think of all the customer calls you could be missing while stuck on the phone for hours hearing all about your sister's latest work problems!

You should definitely arrange at least one dedicated phone line just for your business calls. In an ideal world you would have one line for outgoing calls and another to receive calls, but if that seems excessive at first you could always use the home line to dial out, keeping the business line free for incoming calls from customers ! If possible, splash out on a cordless phone for the business line—at least that way you can keep it near you at all times, and dash to the 'office' for privacy should a call come in while you're making lunch! Make sure also that you have a call-forwarding facility, as well as an answer-phone for calls during out of office hours.

Toll- free or local rate number

Having a toll-free or local-rate number buys you instant credibility with your customers and doesn't have to cost a fortune. Before you sign up for one of these, check the small print—some can only be dialed toll-free or local-rate from land-lines....not ideal if you feel the majority of your customers are mobile users who may be discouraged from calling from their cell.

USA: Talk to your land-line service provider to see what they offer, and also do a search for 800 numbers online. Shop around and you will find a flat-rate plan that ensures you pay a set monthly fee regardless of the volume of calls received.

UK: With an 0845 Local Rate Number, customers can call you from anywhere in the UK at local rate. Many providers also offer call forwarding services, where you can use their online facility to instantly re-route your incoming 0845 number to another mobile or landline whenever you need to (say, in the event that you are out of the office at a craft show and don't want to miss customer calls).

Super-fast broadband connection

As a business owner, you will almost certainly be spending lots of time online - whether it's researching suppliers and craft shows or updating and managing your Etsy store or website—so if you haven't done so already, now is the time to upgrade your internet connection to the speediest available in your area. Because life really is too short to wait 3 minutes for a web page to load!

Email account

You definitely need to have a separate email address for all business dealings. If you want to look professional, you should avoid using the free e-mail servers like hotmail, aol, yahoo or gmail. An email with your domain name is much more business-like.

Once you've registered your domain name, it's easy to add on a 'hosting' account which is a package, usually with a monthly fee, that provides a certain amount of MB of web space to build your website on, and also the ability to create as many email addresses as you need using '*yourname@yourdomainname.com*' as the email address. For instance, you could create '*amy@kidsville.com*' for personal/direct communications, and also '*hello@kidsville.com*', '*returns@kidsville.com*' etc. This way not only can you keep and deal with emails for different business purposes separately, but if at a later date you employ help for certain tasks, it will be easier to route the correct emails to their computer to be dealt with by them.

Digital Camera

Unless you're lucky enough to have a friend or partner who is a real photography whizz, chances are you'll be taking lots of product photos yourself for use on websites, online stores etc.—at least at first. Invest in a good digital camera—it will pay for itself ten times over if it means you can do all your own product photography!

Office Essentials Checklist

- Dedicated 'office' area to work from
- Business phone line, with calling forwarding/answering
- Toll-free or local-rate number
- Fast broadband internet connection
- Computer/laptop
- Printer and scanner
- Dedicated business email address
- Digital camera

What Kind Of Business Are You?

At this stage, there are 3 obvious types of business structures to choose from*:

• Sole Proprietor

• Partnership

• Limited Liability Company (LLC)

*there are various other Corporation options available, but for most small start-ups one of the 3 above would be most likely.

Sole Proprietor

A Sole Proprietor (Sole Trader in the UK) is perhaps the most common way of starting a business for many crafty entrepreneurs. If you're working alone, with no employees, this can be the simplest way to get started. It will mean that your company is unincorporated, and also that you are 100% personally responsible should anything go wrong in the business. If someone became ill or injured as a result of one of your products, then a customer could, in theory, sue you personally. You would also be responsible for any business debts or loans. On the flip side, there's very little paperwork involved when operating as a sole proprietor, and you simply file your taxes as a self-employed individual, much the same as if you were a freelancer. (If you're in the UK you should also register to pay National Insurance payments as a self-employed person, in order to maintain your contributions.)

Partnership

If you're lucky enough to have a like-minded friend to start your business with you may choose to form a partnership. Two heads are better than one, and it can definitely be tons of fun sharing the journey with the right person. Right now, probably the last thing on your mind is "what if we fall out/wish to leave the business/sell our share" etc. But a little planning now can save a big headache in the long run.

What if your business partner has a new baby, just as things are taking off? Have you agreed how much time off she will take? Or, if you're willing to spend 12 hours a day, 7 days a week getting things going, but feel their contribution falls way short of that, how will you deal with it? Different work ethics and expectations can be the downfall of even the best friendships once business and money are in the mix.

You should draft an agreement, in writing, that outlines who is responsible for what, what contribution each will make to the running of the business, the initial investment and % of the company owned by each partner, and what will happen in the event that one partner wants to leave the business.

Be aware though that with a partnership, not only can you be held personally responsible for company debts in the same way as being a Sole Proprietor, but you are also liable for any and all business debts, even those run up by your partner. This 'joint and several liability' means you are each responsible both jointly, and individually, in the event of the other person being unable to pay. So, if your best friend is tons of fun and a great creative asset, but a bit free and easy with the cash, perhaps build into the agreement that any purchases over a certain amount must be agreed by both parties.

Limited Liability Company (LLC)

If you're keen to protect your personal assets from any business dealings, then an LLC could be for you. Many small business owners operate as an LLC as it allows them to keep their business and personal finances completely separate, and offers them personal protection should anything go wrong in business. There is of course more paperwork involved than trading as a Sole Proprietor, but it could be worth it in the long run for peace of mind. An LLC can be owned by an individual or a group of people, so this could also offer a good alternative to a partnership (though still draw up a partnership agreement too).

(In the UK this is called a Limited Company and uses the following—'Ltd.' —after your company name on any official paperwork i.e. 'Kidsville Ltd.'

Note – If you do become a Limited Liability Company, you should always use the 'LLC' or 'Ltd.' at the end of your company name on all official paperwork, letterheads and on your website at the bottom. You don't, however, need to work it into your logo thankfully!

Licenses and Permits

Regardless of whether you're planning on selling your wares online and at a few craft shows, or targeting the big-box stores, if you're selling goods for a profit, then you are considered "in business". Anyone in business needs to have the right license, permits and follow the tax laws for their state or country. Here are a few essentials:

Get A Business License

This is an annual license, usually purchased via your county clerk, that allows you to operate a business within your state.

DBA (Doing Business As)—Fictitious Business Name

Assuming you've given your business its own name, then you will be 'Doing Business' under that name, not your own name, so you need to file a Fictitious Business Name, also called a DBA through your county clerk.

(In the UK, DBA is known as 'Trading As' i.e. 'Amy Smith t/a Kidsville'. While there is nothing to actually file like in the US, your business bank account will be in your 'trading as' name, that way you can accept payments made out to 'Kidsville.')

Business Bank Account

Not only can it be illegal to run your business through your personal bank account, having a separate account for your business will make things way easier when it comes to keeping your personal and business finances separate and for preparing tax returns and filing accounts. You can open the account in the name of your business once you have filed your DBA.

When opening a new account—check the small print for charges. If you think you will be regularly depositing cash (say, after craft shows), choose a bank with a local branch, and also check the fees for each deposit. I always open a second business account for tax money which I put away on a regular basis. As money comes in, I put a proportion away in the second account—this keeps my tax money safe and separate from the day-to-day business funds—a real bonus when it's time to pay tax, you can sleep at night knowing that it is safely tucked away!

Certificate Of Resale

Also known as a Seller's Permit, if you are selling taxable goods, you will need to apply for one of these through the governing body responsible for taxation in your state (check with SCORE if you're unsure where to look). Once you have this, you will be responsible for charging your local state tax on any sales you make, and filing regular tax returns. Any sales you make to people out of your state, or wholesale, are exempt from this tax.

If you want to buy supplies wholesale, then you will need to provide your sellers permit and resale number to qualify. Likewise, when stores wish to buy from you at wholesale, they must show you theirs. So you should apply for this asap before you start purchasing supplies for your first big production run!

UK ONLY—VAT (Value Added Tax)

There is a law in the UK that any company whose turnover exceeds £73,000 per annum must register for VAT. Once registered, the company must charge an additional 20% on all sales, and pay this amount (less any VAT they have paid to other companies) by filing a quarterly VAT return. Business Link have some excellent links for more info on VAT. The VAT rate and threshold can change so always check online at www.hmrc.gov.uk.

Federal Tax ID

Also known as an EIN (Employer Identification Number), this is a number the IRS supplies to most business entities in the US. If your business operates as a partnership, corporation or has any employees then you need to apply for one of these. If you are a Sole Proprietor, then you do not require one—your Social Security number is all that is needed when filing taxes.

Insurance

There are various types of Insurance to consider:

Health Insurance: You may already be covered by your partner's employee-sponsored health plan, but if not it's important to know that you have sufficient cover in the event of illness.

Income Replacement Insurance: What would happen if you were ill and unable to work or run the business? Aimed at self-employed individuals, for a monthly fee—based on the amount of cover and what your usual/desired monthly income amount is—you can insure against being unable to operate due to illness. In the event that you have a serious illness, the insurance would pay out an agreed amount of money per month for a set amount of time.

Product Liability Insurance: This covers you in the event that someone sues you as a result of any injury caused by your product. Now I realize that you may be thinking "I make earrings and necklaces, what could go wrong", and you may well be right. But certain types of handmade items do have the potential for problems—especially skincare items, candles or burners, and anything involving children or children's products. Take advice and protect yourself if necessary.

Trademarks and Intellectual Property

So you have decided on your company name, and you may also have a great name for your main product. While it may seem rather early to start thinking about having such a successful product that others may want to imitate, it's very important to protect yourself right from the beginning.

What is a trademark?

A trademark provides legal protection in the marketplace for the name of your product or business name and/or logo, and is defined as any word, name, symbol or device used to distinguish one producer's goods from others.

A trademark is a key piece of intellectual property (IP) that is vital to the future success of your product or brand. You need to protect your product's name right at the beginning, before you start selling it or introducing it to the marketplace. If you don't, you could risk someone else coming along and registering it and contesting your rights to use that name.

You also need to register it right at the beginning to be absolutely sure that you are not compromising someone else's registered trademark.

It can take up to a year to have your trademark formally approved by the USPTO, so during that time you should use the TM symbol next to your product's name, to let the public know that you are claiming it as your mark.

Searching for and Registering a Trademark
To search for and/or register a trademark, go to the USPTO website www.uspto.gov and click on the Trademarks tab. Under the Basics tab you will find 'Where Do I Start'.

UK readers: You can search for and register trademarks at the Intellectual Property Office www.ipo.gov.uk. There are hundreds of classification categories, so you may have to register your TM in several different categories to ensure full protection.

Protect Yourself!
A google search for 'Trademark Registering' will throw up hundreds of companies offering to file your TM application, often for a considerable fee. Obviously these companies have a level of expertise in dealing with what may at first be an overwhelming and confusing amount of information, but if you want to avoid unnecessary costs it really is worth trying to do this yourself, or asking a business-whizz friend to help!

Let's Get Down To Business!

Creating A Business Plan
Now that all the set-up is done, you can really get this show on the road!

Next up, you'll need to do a business plan. Sounds scary? Well chances are, you've actually already thought about most of the aspects involved and can easily answer many of the questions. And writing a proper business plan can also throw up some really interesting questions that you may not have yet considered.

Think of a business plan simply as a list of questions on a form or template. Deal with each question as it comes up, and see what your response is. Take your time to consider each carefully—you're planning the next few years of your working life after all, so there's no need to rush!

By having those questions and answers in front of you, it can not only help you map the way forward for your business and help you define your goals in real, concrete terms, but it can be an excellent reference tool as your business grows. It's so easy to get caught up in the day-to-day running of a business that we lose sight of our original aims, so once completed you can refer to it often to see if you're on track.

Each chapter of this book will cover a different area from your business plan, so you can refer back to these pages once you've finished reading!

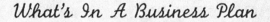

What's In A Business Plan

Company Name

Mission Statement

List of company owners/staff and their responsibilities

Investment cash required at start-up

Location of your business

Initial product Line and Prices

Equipment and materials needed

Production plan for growth

Development of product line and frequency of new products

Target Market

Market Research

Marketing and PR Plan

Financial Plan (including 12 month–3 year budget)

Exit strategy

The great news is that there are tons of free resources out there and many Business Plan templates available.

Free Business Plan Templates

USA

SCORE: Service Corps of Retired Executives
www.score.org/template_gallery.html

SBA: Small Business Administration
www.sba.gov/starting_business/planning/writingplan.html

WBDC: Women's Business Development Center
www2.wbdc.org/tools/develop/develop.asp

UK

Business Link
www.businesslink.org.uk

Getting Help

Starting your own business needn't mean going it alone—there's a huge amount of free help and advice available out there, so make the most of it and you'll soon be on the road to success, and meet some amazing and inspirational people along the way!

SCORE (Service Corps of Retired Executives): SCORE is a nonprofit association dedicated to educating entrepreneurs and helping small businesses start, grow, and succeed across the US. SCORE is a resource partner with the US Small Business Administration (SBA), and has been mentoring small business owners for more than forty years. With a network of over 13,000 volunteer mentors, across 364 local chapters, SCORE also offers local business workshops and tons of free online business tools. More info at www.score.org

SBDC (Small Business Development Center): This is a free program run by the Small Business Administration and is available in every state in the US. Visit their website to find your local office at www.sba.gov

UK: Business Link is a fantastic resource for new and small business owners. With a website full of excellent reference material and online tools and calculators, plus regional offices offering free and discounted one-to-one sessions with small business advisors, it's an invaluable resource for those starting out. Business Link also runs hundreds of local events, seminars and networking opportunities across the country, providing a fantastic way to increase your business skills and meet other entrepreneurs and mentors! www.businesslink.gov.uk

Find A Mentor: Perhaps someone in your circle of friends or contacts already knows a successful crafty entrepreneur who would be willing to meet up for a coffee and a chat. Or maybe you've met someone through a local craft fair or group who impressed you with what they've achieved with their business already. Practical advice from someone who has already been through what you're embarking on and has lived to tell the tale is worth its weight in gold.

Free Business Templates

Available To Download From SCORE
www.score.org/template_gallery.html

Business Plan for a Start-Up Business

Business Plan for an Established Business

Balance Sheet (Projected)

Bank Loan Request for Small Business

Breakeven Analysis

Cash Flow Statement (12 months)

Competitive Analysis

Financial History & Ratios

Loan Amortization Schedule

Nondisclosure Agreement

Opening Day Balance Sheet

Personal Financial Statement

Projected Balance Sheet

Profit & Loss Projection (12 months)

Profit & Loss Projection (3 years)

Sales Forecast (2 months)

Start-up Expenses

Checklist

- Set up your home office area
- Get a dedicated phone line
- Order a toll-free or local rate number
- Upgrade internet connection if necessary
- Trademark your company or product name
- Decide on your company legal structure and register accordingly
- Open a business bank account
- Get a business license
- Apply for a seller's permit
- Apply for federal tax ID (if required)
- Insurance
- Business plan

Relax!
**Give yourself a pat on the back—
you are now officially IN BUSINESS!**

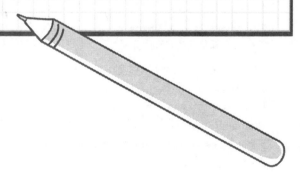

Chapter 4

The Price Is Right!

Production and Pricing

So you know what you want to make—you may even have been making these on a small to medium scale already—and you know exactly what materials you need to make them. Now it's time to think like a businessperson and figure out exactly how much it costs you to make each item. And how many can you realistically make each day/week/month on your own.

It's likely that so far you've been buying your materials in fairly small quantities from local stores or online, paying full 'retail' prices. You may even already have an idea of roughly how much it costs to make one item. But if you really wanted to scale things up and start seriously selling your wares, it's time to look at your costs in a lot more detail so that you know exactly what your potential profit margins are, and figure out how many, and at what price, you need to sell each month to make a decent living.

So if you've figured out how much it costs you to make 1 handbag, what about the cost of producing 50 handbags? If you suddenly had an order for 1000 bags, would you know where to get 1000 of the exact handles that you used before, and enough of the fabric that the original bags were made in? This is where sourcing comes in. It could be time to find some new suppliers who can accommodate your needs as your business and production numbers grow, and provide all the materials that you need, on a regular basis, at a great price.

In this chapter we're going to look at:

- **Sourcing** – how to find all the components you need at the best prices.

- **Packaging** – some tips on choosing the best packaging for you and the retailer!

- We'll calculate your **COGS** (that's Cost Of Goods Sold by the way!).

- We'll also look at the best ways to arrive at the right **Retail and Wholesale Price** for your products.

- And let's not forget **Production**—making those products—calculating the time spent on each item, and, when it's time to grow and take on extra help, the real cost of employing others to make your products.

The following pages should help you create all the figures you'll need to move forward and add to your business plan, and help you prepare for the next steps in your business journey!

Sourcing

Sourcing: *'a process of searching for and qualifying potential vendors of services or supplies essential to the operation of your business, then negotiating with them to arrive at a successful and profitable working relationship.'*
Or, as I like to say: 'Finding the stuff I need to make my products, at the best prices!'

Why Buy Wholesale?

Say it currently costs you around $4.50 to make each handbag, using fabric and handles purchased in smallish quantities...but what if you could commit to buying, say, 1000 of those handles, and entire bolts of the fabrics, then you could really bring those prices down significantly. Obviously this all requires cash, and the confidence to believe that you really can use/sell all of the resulting stock. But if you're dreaming big, and planning for bigger, then buying wholesale is the way to go. You may be currently paying $2.30 for a bag clasp in your local craft store, but find the right supplier and commit to a larger quantity like 500 or 1000 and that price could come right down to less than a dollar a unit. And if you could reduce your fabric costs from $3.50 to $1.59 a yard buy buying by the bolt from a fabric wholesaler, then you've significantly reduced the cost of each bag to less than half of the original costing. This not only gives you far more profit when selling directly to the public, but could make it possible to also wholesale to stores and still have enough of a profit margin to make it worthwhile.

Can you Replicate?

You may be making beautiful necklaces using recycled vintage costume jewelry sourced from garage sales, or unique purses using vintage fabrics, but if you intend to wholesale, could you lay your hands on enough fabric or components for an order of 500, at fairly short notice? While I'm not suggesting you scrap your unique components for generic beads and fabrics, or compromise your creative vision, it's worth thinking about what you would do if 'the best happened' and your products were selling like hot-cakes. Could you keep up with the demand? Could you perhaps mix the found materials with really cool 'vintage style' components to create new designs that are much easier to produce in larger volumes?

What is a Vendor?

A vendor is basically anyone who provides a service or supply to another. So vendors you use could be anyone from your fabric or findings supplier, to the printing company who produce your business cards or flyers. Likewise, when you start supplying to stores, they will consider you one of their many 'vendors'.

Finding The Right Vendors

These days, everything you could possibly need can be found online. Can you imagine how difficult things would have been 10 or 15 years ago—ploughing through phone directories, cold calling hundreds of companies to find the right suppliers. Now, at the click of a mouse you can search for whatever you need from the comfort of your desk (or armchair!)

As well as the usual online search engines, there are many online business directories that can help in your search.

Thomasnet.com
ThomasNet is a hugely comprehensive online search tool for products and services. You can use it to search for manufacturers and suppliers in the US and worldwide. And with over 67,000 product and service categories, you should be able to find just about anything. You simply type in the product or service you're looking for, and a list of suitable companies appears. You can narrow the search field to your country or state, then click through to each company website to see what they offer.

Alibaba.com
Alibaba is very similar to ThomasNet, with listings from thousands of suppliers from across the globe. You can search by product description, category and even country, to narrow it down to local suppliers.

There are also hundreds of other international sites, many featuring product manufacturers in the Far East, but at this stage it probably makes sense to stick to a supplier close to home until you really need the huge volumes it would require to make importing from abroad cost-effective.

What To Look For In a Vendor

Once you've narrowed down your search to 3 or 4 possible vendors, it's time to call each of them with a few questions. How they deal with you, a potential new customer, at this early stage will give you a good indication of whether this is the kind of company you'd like to be working with. Working with vendors is closer to a partnership than a typical seller/customer relationship, as you both need to be able to rely on the other.

They need to feel confident that you are a good prospect, and that you have the potential to become a top customer of theirs. This encourages them to give you the best possible price, and to make the effort to meet your deadlines for supply of products. So it's important to approach each call to a potential new vendor with confidence, and to be ready to sell yourself and your fantastic company and successful products! If your company is still in the early stages, you need to make them believe that there is a real benefit to them in doing business with you. Your success will become their success!

Likewise, you need to feel confident, not only that you are getting a good deal on your purchases, but that they will be a reliable source of product. I had a couple of vendors who started off great, promising prompt, on-demand supplies of some of the key components of my kits, only for there to be serious supply issues further down the line. Deliveries were delayed, answers to when a product would be back in stock increasingly vague, and I was left scrabbling around trying to find an alternative supplier at the last minute, with a large order to fulfil and not enough parts to complete it. I quickly learned my lesson and from that point on made sure I had 2 or 3 suppliers of each component, so that I always had a fall-back option in the event my main supplier let me down.

Don't be afraid to negotiate. Often the first price they quote you may be their opening offer. There's no harm in asking if that really is their best price, or if that can be reduced if/when you commit to greater volumes etc. Many suppliers may even already have price bands in place, so you can calculate your costings based on buying 500, 1000, 5000 units and so on. That way you can factor in these economies of scale to future orders and production runs.

So, I really believe that there isn't a better way to invest your time at the start of your company than finding the right vendors.

Sourcing *101*

Price: Price is king. Paying even a few pennies more on each item can have a real effect on your profit margins, so negotiate hard and shop around for the best price.

Quality: Often, there's no such thing as a bargain, and while one supplier may offer a cheaper price, is the item up to the quality standards you require? Quality vs. price is a fine balancing act.

Availability: The cheapest supplier in the world is no use to you if they cannot supply regular stocks of the items you most need. Discuss availability—how long does it take them to re-stock items once they sell out? If your preferred wholesaler orders in huge quantities from the Far East, you could be in for a long wait before the next shipment arrives. Building a good relationship with a vendor involves letting them know which items you need them to keep in stock, and them being confident it is worth keeping these items in stock as they know for sure your next order is on the way.

Reliability: Will you have a regular rep or point-person to deal with at your supplier? How do you find them? Do they email over the price lists or initial information promptly and return your calls the same day? Or are they tricky to get hold of, and full of excuses for delays. Never a good sign!

Packaging

For some, packaging can almost be an afterthought, but how you package and present your products can often be crucial to its success.

Visit a craft show and while you may find 2 vendors, each selling similarly beautiful bath products, chances are it's the one with the beautiful packaging that will have a line of customers. While one vendor may have added simple white sticky labels from her printer to each jar or pot bearing the name of the contents, believing that the product itself was enough to guarantee sales, the other may have gone that extra mile.

Customers love a beautifully presented item, so the vintage-style jars adorned with retro gingham ribbons, recycled paper bags and a retro boudoir-style booth made the other vendor's products super appealing and really stand out from the crowd. Placed into sweet brown paper bags and wrapped in beautiful tissue, customers were queuing up for her cute and inexpensive treats.

It's What's Inside That Counts

Good packaging obviously counts, but it should also reflect the contents. The previous vendor chose a retro style packaging for her bath goods, which made perfect sense and beautifully matched the contents of her bath products containing traditional scents, with names like 'Lavender Lafayette', or 'Relaxing Rose Foot Balm'. Had her products been more like 'Marguerita Madness Fizzing Bath Bombs' or 'Tingling Tequila Tootsie Cream', then maybe a more modern, fresh style of packaging, would have been more appropriate!

Will It Work In-Store?

If your aim is to ultimately sell your products into retailers, it's crucial to think like a retailer and how they display products similar to yours. Before I even decided on the packaging for my craft kits, I visited not only the main national department store that I dreamed of my kits being stocked in (and they were, gracing their shelves less than 9 months later!), but also many smaller independent stores who could be my potential customers. I quickly saw that my initial idea of having my kits in a box was flawed. These stores all featured craft kits hanging on hooks on a wall, as it made the most use of their limited space, and most of the kits came either in a clear hanger bag, or a gift-style paper bag with rope handles. So all kits needed to be 'hangable'. On closer inspection I noted that those kits in a gift-style bag had the actual kit contents in a sealed clear bag within the gift bag to keep all the contents together, and a picture of the kit itself as a sticker on the front of the main gift bag. Where the gift bag had been sealed with a sticker at the top, members of the public had burst this open in a bid to view the contents inside. So the gift bags ended up looking ripped or damaged, and ultimately would not sell. The kits I liked best were in clear A4 sized hanger bags, with the picture of the item to the front, and then the customer could turn it around and view the contents at the back. The bags were sealed, but as the customer could easily see what fabrics were in the kit, there were no damages. So it was a no-brainer for me. Clear hanger bags it was!

Can I Ship It? (Yes, You Can!)

While I fully planned to be wholesaling my kits to lots of retailers, I also knew that I would be selling them online and having to ship orders all over the world. This was another reason the light, flat, clear bags were a great choice for my kits. They could easily fit into a large padded envelope, and were light and secure enough to post. Had I stuck with my original box idea, not only would the packaging itself cost 4 times as much per kit, I would then have had to buy expensive thicker boxes to ship them in too, and the weight and shipping costs would also have been higher.

When I received my first order from the major national retailer, it was for over 1000 kits. Luckily, the clear hanger bags meant that I could fit 50 kits into a large cardboard box, so the order shipped as around 24 boxes. Had I opted for boxes or gift bags as kit packaging, only around 12 would have fitted into each large box...so I would have had to pay for 100 large boxes to be shipped. That would have wiped out any profits right away!

So, if you're planning to sell online, or to retailers, think about how easy to package your finished item would be, and whether the added weight or size—like a glass jar, or large box, could make shipping to customers prohibitively expensive.

Cost Per Unit

As with every single component of whatever you are making to sell, the cost per unit of your packaging is crucial. An extra dollar per unit spent on packaging could, in real terms, raise your retail price by around $3.00. So, as you work out your COGS (coming next), it's important to figure out the maximum you can afford to spend on packaging and find clever and creative ways to deliver a beautifully packaged product on a budget!

Inspiration

Look around at similar products to yours—how are they packaged? If I hadn't visited those retailers and gone ahead with custom printed boxes for my kits, I could have made a very expensive mistake. Visit stores, and see where you think your product would fit in the store, which department and even your 'fantasy' location within that department. Or if you're aiming at small independent boutiques, see how they are displaying similar items? Not only will this help you figure out the best packaging, the ingenious ways retailers display their stock could give you some great inspiration for your own displays at future craft and trade shows!

Think Like A Retailer

When I finally got my meeting with the buyer at the big department store chain, she was impressed with my knowledge of their stores and products, and the reasons why I had opted for the packaging I did. She confessed that she secretly hated the 'gift-bag' style of kit packaging—there were too many damages and the cardboard bags were easily bashed and damaged and soon new stock could end up looking worn and dated and therefore impossible to sell.

She confirmed that often the packaging, and how it can be displayed in-store, is as much a consideration when buying a product as the product itself. Retailers hate fragile packaging that can be damaged in transit. Often, goods have to be shipped across the country, usually to their central distribution warehouse, then handled several times as they cross the supply chain and finally end up on a shop floor.

And half the time, it's the actual customers who can be the source of many problems for suppliers and retailers! Some people love to rip or force open packaging in a bid to get a better look at the product inside—packaging YOU may have spent ages lovingly creating for each item! So, let's make it easy on them. Include all the right images and information ON the packaging, and try to troubleshoot any potential ways your packaging could be damaged or mishandled.

Packaging Must-Haves

- Clear image of contents
- Always include company name, logo and website URL.
- Usually on rear: Description of Goods, contents, ingredients, weights, safety information, age suitability, does it contain small parts and not suitable for small children etc.
- Washing/fabric care instructions
- Space for price sticker or barcode.

DIY vs. Custom print

If your packaging is fairly simple—say a cool hanger tag to attach to the handle of your handbags, you can probably create something yourself on your computer. With some basic design skills, some quality card-stock and a good printer, you may have all the tools you need.

If you have something slightly fancier in mind, the great news is that with digital printing, it's finally possible to do short print runs at a fairly good price. Always think economies of scale. If you want a square box featuring your logo and fancy design to house your homemade lip balms, get creative to find a way to use one generic box and add a separate label with the 'flavor', yourself as you package each balm. That way you can order 1000 of the same box and adapt it for each flavor in the range— a much better option of doing short print runs per flavor, or having to pay for 6 print runs of 1000 or more different boxes! Having an entirely different custom printed piece of packaging for every single item in your range could prove a huge outlay that you could do without!

COGS – Cost of Goods Sold

This is the amount of money you spend to make the products you sell. This is usually figured as a percentage of the selling price i.e if you sell a purse at $10 and it costs you $5 to make, you have a 50% COGS.

Say, for instance you make cute fabric coin purses. You will probably start off making no more than a couple of hundred at a time if you have a craft fair selling directly to the public coming up. But it's good to calculate at this early stage how much they would cost to make if you did get a big order and/or could afford to buy your materials in bulk. Seeing the difference in the COGS could really spur you on to commit to some bulk supplies to really bring your unit price down.

	Bulk pricing description	Cost (1–100 units)	Bulk Buy Cost (over 1000)
MATERIALS			
Fabric for outer	$4.95 per yard or $2.69/yard bulk wholesale 8 purses/yard	$0.62	$0.34
Fabric for lining	$2.95/yard or $1.49 bulk 8 purses / yard	$0.37	$0.19
Clasp for purse	$3.49 each for up to 250 or $1.24 for 1000 units.	$3.49	$1.24
Custom fabric tag with logo	$12.00/100 £69/1000	$0.12	$0.07
Clear plastic packing bag	$7.00/100 $25.00/1000	$0.07	$0.03

	Bulk pricing description	Cost (1–100 units)	Bulk Buy Cost (over 1000)
Custom sticker	$40/1000 (min quantity)	$0.04	$0.04
Cost of Materials (A)		$4.81	$1.91
LABOR			
	Cutting Fabric 1 hour = 100 panels. 2 panels (exterior & lining)/purse. Pay help $10/hour*. 50 bags = $10.	$.20	$.20
	Sewing and Fitting Clasp: approx 4 bags/ hour@$10/hour	$2.50	$2.50
	Packing and stickering 200/hour	$0.05	$0.05
Cost of Labor (B)		$2.75	$2.75
TOTAL COGS (A&B)		**$7.56/purse**	**$4.66/purse**

We'll look at employing help in **Chapter 8**, but for the purposes of this COGS exercise I've calculated paying someone $10/hour to assist you making your 'purses'. Clearly this will vary with each individual/ country/situation!

Pricing Your Products

If you've already been selling your crafty items, you may have a good idea of what people are willing to pay for your creations. If you've not yet taken that step, it's time for a bit more market research to see how much people may be willing to pay for what you are producing. This can be harder than it sounds, especially if what you're offering is pretty unusual or requires a lot of time to make. Say you're making purses. No two purses are the same, but you may see purses of similar quality in a high-end boutique on sale for $69. Does this mean that you can charge a similar amount? Not necessarily. If your products are incredibly high quality, maybe leather and hand-stitched, and you're happy selling a couple at a time to rare high-end boutiques then fine.

But realistically it's unlikely you could charge that amount at a typical craft show or direct to the public online. Once you have your product samples ready, show them to as many people as you can and ask "How much would you be willing to pay for something like this." Now some of the answers may be frustrating—not everyone realizes the time and effort that goes into handmade goods and they can be quick to compare the price of cheap mass produced chain-store purses with your lovingly hand-crafted one of a kind vintage fabric purse—but the feedback could prove very interesting.

Say you discovered that most people are in agreement that they would happily part with between $14.95 and $19.95 for your little purses.

Setting a Retail Price

Armed with a rough guide to how much you could be selling your purses to the public for, it's time to check that there's enough potential profit in it to make things worthwhile for you. You should aim for at least 100% mark-up, more if possible. So, looking at your pricing grid, if your COGS is $7.56, multiply that by 2 and you get $15.12. Not far off a $14.95 price point. Multiply it by the ideal mark-up of 2.5 and you get $18.90, even better! So, making in small-ish quantities and selling directly to the public is a definite option. Hurrah!

Setting a Wholesale Price

Before you finalise your retail price point, let's see if you can also realistically make these purses at a price that you can wholesale them to other retailers and still make some profit.

If the maximum retail price point for your purses is $19.95 then let's look at whether you can afford to sell them wholesale to retailers. They will expect to pay you no more than $10 per purse, probably even less. If you continued to buy your materials in small quantities, it would cost you $7.56 —leaving not much of a profit margin for you. However, if you secured a decent wholesale order and had the cash-flow to commit to buying your materials in bulk, by bringing your COGS down to $4.66 per purse, that's over 100% mark-up for you. Excellent.

How Retailers work: Margins and Mark-ups

Smaller retailers tend to operate on a typical 100% mark-up basis, i.e if they buy an item from you for $10, they need to be able to sell it for at least $20 to achieve their margins.

Big retailers use a slightly more complicated formula—one which completely bamboozled me when I first came across it (and each big retailer may well have their own formula, just to keep things interesting!).

Retail Price Point (R), minus the cost of purchasing wholesale (W), equals X. Then X is divided by the Retail Price Point (R).

$$R-W=X/R$$

So if your purse has a $20 Retail Price Point (R), minus your $10 wholesale cost (W) = $10 (X).

$$X/R \text{ is } \$10/\$20 = 0.5 \text{ or } 50\% \text{ markup}$$

But did you, as I did, think, "Hang on a minute. I thought selling it to them at $10, for them to sell to the public at $20, meant a 100% mark-up?" Yep? Confusing, isn't it!?

Most big retailers will demand more than a 50% mark-up, many want 60% ideally.

In the UK, standard mark-up for small stores is wholesale x 2.4. (This allows for VAT @ 20%). So for a £20 purse they would expect to pay £8.33 plus VAT (£8.33 x 2.4 = £20). If you are not Vat registered you would just charge £8.33. National chains have a similarly complicated formula to US stores, and vary depending on the company.

The Final Word On Pricing

With a much larger profit margin to be had by selling to the public rather than wholesaling, many crafters choose to stick with direct sales rather than try to sell to retailers. There's absolutely nothing wrong with this strategy, and it can certainly work for those who want to keep their business at a manageable level and not invest too much time or cash, but grow organically.

On the one hand, you may think, "Why sell a purse to retailers for only a few dollars profit when I can sell it directly and make 3 times as much profit?" But then again, when you consider the overheads of the booth cost, 3 days of your life spent at a craft fair plus all the preparation time etc, you may not actually be much better off if you had been overseeing a production run of lots of purses from the comfort of your own workshop. Also, shipping hundreds of units at a time, instead of lots of small, individual orders is a much more cost-efficient use of your time. Being stocked in the right retailers can be a good way to develop your brand and get your name out and ultimately lead more customers directly to your own website too—so it can work well for you on many levels!

I used to include a promotional flyer with a free shipping offer or discount code inside all of my kits that I wholesaled. The hope was that people may well buy the first kit in a store, but then be encouraged to visit my website and buy directly next time!

One last tip: Once you do start selling to stores, I'd strongly advise against undercutting the recommended Retail Price. If stores are selling your purses at $19.95, they won't be happy to discover that you are selling them on your own website, or at fairs, for just $14.95. So it's time to set an RRP and have not only each new retailer agree to that within your terms of sale (more of this later), but stick to it yourself.

Chapter

5

PR and Marketing

PR & Marketing

Marketing and PR are the essential tools in making your potential customers aware that you exist! You could have the best product in the world, but unless people know that it is available, and how they can purchase it, you could never make a single sale!

Whether or not you think you already have the skills to become a successful 'marketeer', if you're passionate about your products, and want to sell as many of them as possible, then so many aspects of 'marketing and pr' will be things that you instinctively want to do anyway. If you love what you do, and are proud of the work that you're creating, why wouldn't you want to shout it from the rooftops?

I personally never leave the house without a stack of business cards in my bag—and when I was launching my first craft business I quickly distributed over 5,000 flyers with the help of family and friends, and literally walked the streets spreading the word, such was my passion and determination to make a success of my new venture!

The Secret Success Formula!
Idea/product = 5%
Passion and Marketing = 95%

A good Marketing and PR campaign will identify the type of people you want to reach, and find both obvious and inventive ways of reaching them. Whilst large companies have equally large marketing budgets, the smaller company or crafty entrepreneur must look to find ways to reach their customers that is cost effective and within their limited budget.

The ultimate aim is obviously to sell your products. Unless you have an unlimited budget to throw at paid advertising, you'll need to have a 'think outside the box' attitude—and plenty of determination. You need to approach a broad range of people to let them know all about your new company and fabulous products—and about you too! No time to become a shrinking violet, sometimes you may find that the local paper is interested in running a story about a new, local company like yours, with the entire article based around you…they love the human angle!

Marketing: This involves the use of advertisements, leaflets, flyers, newsletters and other profile-raising means to target your customers.

PR: Public Relations covers the use of the media to make your customers aware of your product or service. Magazines, newspapers, TV and radio (both national and local) are all key ways of gaining exposure.

Online PR and Social Networking: The use of facebook, twitter, blogs and websites to reach potential customers. The opportunities to promote yourself and your products online are endless, with a worldwide reach! In fact, such is the power of Social Networking that I've dedicated the whole of Chapter 6 to Social Media and Online PR!

Marketing and PR Tools

Before you even begin to start 'PR-ing' yourself, you'll need to get all the right tools and information ready. As the old saying goes, "You only get one chance to make a first impression," and approaching magazines or journalists before you're ready, and without the right tools, could mean they fail to take you (or take your calls!) seriously in the future. Most journalists are bombarded with hundreds of press releases and new products every single week, so being organized, having and offering up all the tools they need to easily mention your product, and dealing with them in a professional and efficient manner will give you a real head start!

Your marketing and PR Tool Kit

- Business cards
- Quality Product Photos
- Product Brochure
- Press Release

- Online presence (see Chapter 6)
- Product samples

Business Cards

So you're at a friend's birthday party, and as luck would have it, the friendly, stylish woman you've been chatting to over a margarita mentions that she works at a very cool magazine. She asks what you do, and you dazzle her with the details of your exciting new business and products... "Wow, that sounds like just the kind of thing we regularly feature in our marketplace pages—do you have a business card?" Well, do you? Now that you're a high flying crafty entrepreneur, you'll hopefully find yourself in plenty of situations where people ask for your details, so they can stay in touch, or look up your website. So you should definitely arm yourself with some great business cards.

You can easily design your business cards yourself, or there are tons of online tools with easy templates. Make sure the design and feel of your business cards fit in with your overall branding too. You can even consider featuring an image of your key product on the reverse.

My favorite new site for business cards is www.moo.com. You can choose from hundreds of cool images, funky rounded corner style cards, recycled paper, or even upload your own images so that your business cards feature your very own product images! Feel free to go mad and order a few hundred, after all, you'll soon be networking like crazy, right?

Quality Product Images

If you're planning to sell your products online in any way, then good product photography should be high up on your to-do list. When selling online, and also aiming to have your products featured in magazines, great photos are crucial. If you're planning on showing at trade fairs and wholesaling to retailers, you'll also need to create a good product catalog or brochure for them to take away, so you'll also need some great images for this.

If you're lucky, you may already know a budding amateur photographer who is willing to help you out—if so, grab them with both hands and organise a shoot to get all of your products done in one day to make the most of their time. Don't know anyone? How about checking out any local colleges that run photography courses? You could post a flyer, or speak to the course tutor and bag yourself a willing student who is happy to add to their portfolio!

Failing that, a good quality digital camera and a bit of time and patience will do the job!

Your aim is to have several photos of each product—imagine if a magazine agreed to use a pic of your handmade purse—would you have one great image that gets across the fabulousness and the detail, all in one clear shot? As well as one clear product image, you should also take several other shots that can be used in your online store, so that customers can view various angles and close-ups of any lovely details.

Again, research and inspiration can be a massive help. Check out similar products on other websites and online stores and see how they are shot.

Most high quality magazines will only consider using images that are high resolution, usually 300dpi or higher. DPI means 'Dots Per Inch' and is the industry standard for printing, and 300dpi is the most used as it allows photos within magazines or brochures to be printed clearly.

So make sure your photographer knows this, or set your digital camera to the highest quality setting.

Once you have your high-resolution photos, you may see that because they are such high quality, each photo could be a file size of 3 or 4 MB each. Not only can such large files take ages to upload to online stores and the likes of your Etsy store, but sending several of these at a time via email can cause problems too.

Under no circumstances send a load of high resolution images to someone without them requesting it. As anyone with a blackberry or other email enabled phone may know, someone sending you an email with 20MB of attachments on it can play havoc with your inbox, either clogging up or crashing your emails for the day!

I like to shoot all my images at high-res, then create a new set of low resolution ones for using on websites or emailing for people to view first. You can do this easily at sites like www.shrinkpictures.com.

You can upload the high-res shot then choose to save it at a much lower file size, then use these lower resolution images to send to people, or to drop into press releases—they can still be viewed on their computer perfectly clearly but without the enormous file size of the high-res ones!

Product Images *101*

- Use plain, simple backgrounds – people need to see the product, not the background
- Use natural light, as flash can distort the colors
- Take photos from several different angles to see what works best
- Take close-up shots of any key details or features of your product
- Avoid shadows or direct lighting
- Make sure you have that one clear, bright, killer shot of each product
- Make sure you shoot in high resolution – 300dpi is required for most magazines
- Never send lots of high-res attachments without checking with the recipient first!

Product Catalog or Brochure

Now you're operating as a proper business, you'll need some printed materials to give out to new and prospective customers to remind or introduce them to your business and products.

In the early days, you may decide you just need something cheap and simple to give out to customers at craft fairs to remind them of your products and online store details. In this case, a simple postcard will suffice, with a great image of one of your key products on the front, and website, logo and company info on the rear.

If you're already aiming higher and looking to get magazine coverage, or show at trade fairs, then you'll probably need a more detailed 'product catalog' showing your entire range. Whether you're sending a press kit to a journalist at a local or national magazine, or details of your new products to a buyer for a store, when you need to let people know about your product and you can't see them in person, you need a great printed catalog or flyer showing all your products and information.

As well as a great photo of each product, your catalog should include a brief product description, color and/or size options and 'item numbers'. I always create a separate price list so that in the event your prices change, your expensive catalogs are not rendered outdated or useless.

Product Catalog 101

- Clear image of each product
- Brief product description next to each image
- Size and color options
- Website URL and contact details.

Unless you're already a design whizz, this is where you may need to spend some cash having your catalog professionally designed. Remember, this will be your 'shop window' for buyers and journalists, so it's important that you take the time to produce something special.

Before you even begin to create your catalog, look around at other companies and see how they present their products. Visit craft and trade shows and gather some literature and you'll quickly get a good idea of the kind of quality expected. If you're not quite ready to wholesale, and you already have a great online store featuring all the product images , descriptions and prices, then a more basic double-sided flyer with various images and website details could do for now. These flyers are also cheap enough to give away and use for lots of local marketing ideas—more of which later—so you can easily commit to a decent print run, say 5000, safe in the knowledge that you'll soon use them up spreading the word!

Approaching Magazines and Newspapers

Getting your products featured in magazines is the holy grail of every crafty entrepreneur! Not only is it FREE, but it's been proven time and again that editorial content has hugely more impact on sales than any paid advertising could ever hope to achieve. I know this first hand, as I managed to secure tons of press coverage for my products over the years. Sure, I was lucky enough to have come from a PR background, so I had a real head start, but I'm happy to share my tips here, and with a bit of luck and a lot of perseverance you could soon be spotting your very own products on the pages of a glossy magazine!

Don't be intimidated by the thought of approaching magazines: remember, these people *WANT* to write about interesting people and products, that's their job! It's your job to convince them that, out of the hundreds of other options, they should write about YOU!

Monthly Magazines

There are many different ways to get featured in the big, mainstream magazines. It all depends on each magazine, but in any typical glossy womens monthly there could be more than one area of the magazine that you could realistically aim to be included in. Many magazines do "We Did It" type features, a real-people feature with maybe 3 women who... risked everything to start their own business...or turned a disaster into an opportunity to change their life...or who are launching ethical products. You get the idea. Do you have an interesting story? Then there are the Marketplace pages, the ones where all the hot new 'must have' items are featured. This is where you should be aiming for an image and details of your key product to be mentioned.

Different staff will be responsible for each section of the magazine, so it's important that you target the right person. There's no point pitching a real life story to the marketplace editor, or sending the features editor details of your latest handbag design, they'll simply delete your email and move on.

At the front of each magazine is what's called a 'masthead'—this is the list of staff and their positions at the magazine. At first glance, there may be 40 or more people listed! Who should you be contacting?! Have a good read through the magazine, as often particular sections, like the marketplace pages, may even have 'Edited by' on the opening page. Magazines often outsource some of their feature writing to freelance journalists, so just because a great '3 Women Who...' piece was written by Betsy Williams, she may be based on the other side of the country, so trying to contact her via the magazine could prove fruitless. Often it's either the Features Editor or Commissioning Editor who actually decides on and oversees these types of features.

How to make contact with the right people?

Well, first up, you need to get the email addresses of each of the people you wish to contact. These are rarely listed on the masthead, as few journalists want to make it too easy for hundreds of random readers to contact them! I have 2 tricks for hunting these down.

1) Check other areas of the masthead, as usually the advertising department, who DO want lots of potential advertisers to email them, will list their address. So maybe sam.jones@condenast.com is listed. Great—now you know that the magazine uses the name.surname@companyname.com formula. Should be pretty easy to figure out your target editor's email address from there.

2) To double check the above, or if you still have no clue, call the main switchboard number. Simply say, "I'm having trouble emailing Sally Bird, can I just double check I have the right email address please." Either they will then volunteer it, or you blag it by reading out something like "is it 'sally.bird@themagazine.com?'" No? Then sit back as they give you the correct address. Hopefully!

Now it's time to drop that editor a line, with a short, polite email about your wonderful new product, asking if they would like you to send them a sample. I usually wait 4 days before chasing—when you're a busy market editor a week can pass in a flash—and it's a fine line between reminding someone and annoying them with constant emails!

If they do respond, double check the address on their email signature—many of the big national magazines have several offices, but only one may be featured on the masthead, so don't always assume every editor is based there. Check their address before mailing anything.

When sending stuff to editors, I keep it short and sweet—a handwritten note on your company letterhead or the back of one of your gorgeous postcards, politely asking them to consider mentioning your product, copies of any previous press mentions, along with a brief explanation of your company, a sample of your product and of course the web address where readers can find and purchase the product. You definitely need this to be mentioned to ensure the coverage results in sales! Also include your business card in case they need to contact you for images or more details.

Sometimes it can be tempting just to do a massive 'blind' mail-out, sending samples to a ton of editors in the hope they'll be so dazzled by your product that they'll decide to feature it. Go ahead if you have plenty of product to spare, but in my experience, if they like your email and the initial image of your product, then they'll ask for a sample. If they haven't come back to you after a couple of emails, they're not interested.

Start Small

If the thought of calling up Marie Claire magazine about your handmade purses is just too scary at this stage, why not try some of the more indie or crafty publications. They tend to be more accessible, and chances are better you'll actually land contact with an editor. Dealing with these smaller magazines will help you learn how the process works and you'll be better prepared for when the editor from a larger publication contacts you.

Or—take one small step—choose just four or five magazines that you would and could like to see you or your products in. Ask politely if they'd allow you to send them a sample or tell your story. See what happens!

Local Press

You already live in your area so should be familiar with any local magazines or newspapers. These publications are always keen to feature local people doing interesting things, so you could pitch them a feature about your new company launch. Even better, give them a 'hook to hang it on' like the fact that you are showing at a forthcoming local craft fair—that way readers will be encouraged to come along and visit your booth! These journalists are an important part of ensuring your local profile, so it's vital to strike up a great working relationship with them.

What's a Lead Time?

In the magazine and newspaper world, a lead-time is basically how far in advance of publication a magazine will create the contents. And, confusingly, with most monthly magazines, the date on the cover is usually a month ahead of the on-the-shelf date! For example, the 'June' issue may actually hit the shelves in early May. The magazine may need to be finished and off to the printers by early April, therefore in order to pitch something to the magazine for inclusion in their June issue, you'd need to be approaching them around early March or even sooner!

So you have to think ahead and consider if the press release you are sending will be relevant when the magazine is published. If you have some great red, white & blue products that would work well in a 4th of July themed issue, which may be out in the June, you will need to start approaching magazines in March! So forward planning is vital!

Smaller local magazines and newspapers will have a much shorter lead-time to a glossy magazine, perhaps anything from 3 days to 3 weeks, so no point in approaching them way too soon, you need to do your research and pick your time…all designed to keep you on your toes! The general rule is that the bigger and fancier a publication, the longer the lead-time!

Press Plan!

- Get together a list of all the suitable publications and get a copy of each to have a good read through.
- Now decide where in that magazine you or your products could be mentioned or featured.
- Check the masthead for details of who oversees each section. That way, when you speak with a journalist, you know exactly where you need to be mentioned in the magazine.
- Get the email address of each journalist.
- Only send a sample when requested.
- Keep emails short, sweet and ALWAYS spell-check!
- And, it goes without saying, don't just contact journalists when you're asking for something, an email or cute handmade card with "Thank you so much for the wonderful piece," is always gratefully received!

It's not bragging if you can back it up.
Muhammad Ali

Create a Media Database

I highly recommend creating an Excel spreadsheet or, if you prefer, a simple word document with a table, to create a database of all the media people you will be approaching and hopefully dealing with. As you research each magazine and compile the relevant information and contact details, add this to your database, together with details of all contact you make with them, and any responses from each journalist. You will refer and add to this list time and time again, and it's really helpful to have all the information in one place.

Organise your list with all the monthlies (with the longest lead-times) at the top, working down to newspapers and short-lead publications.

Media Database Essentials

Create a column each for:

- Magazine / newspaper title
- Lead-times and frequency of publication
- Name of Section you wish to target (could be several per mag i.e features, marketplace, advertising)
- Name of person for each section
- Email and phone number for each contact
- Date and details of first contact you made (i.e. Sep 24th 2012, emailed)
- Date and details of 2nd and 3rd follow-up
- Responses
- Outcome (hopefully this will become filled with "Product —USA clutch bag—to be featured in Feb 2013 issue" type mentions!)
- Press cutting received (i.e. do you now have a copy of the piece that ran for your files)

How To Write A Press Release

Your press kit will be a package of all the information on your products and company that you send to journalists, often along with a sample of your key product, in the hope of convincing them to include you in their publication.

Magazine editors and journalists are generally very busy people. They get tons and tons of unsolicited samples and products filling their in-trays on a daily basis, so it's important that your press kit not only stands out from the crowd and reflects your brand, but that it contains all the information they may need if they decide to feature your product.

A press kit will consist of a press release, company biography, product brochure and copies of any previous press clippings you've gained, plus a sample of your product. Your press release may be the first thing they glance at, so it's important that it is short, punchy, interesting, and covering all the key information. Here's a standard format for press releases:

Press Release

- Company logo at top, or on letterhead if you have it
- The words 'For Immediate Release'
- Headline that grabs their attention and summarizes the press release i.e. "Top New York Stylist Launches Hot New Handbag Range"
- Place line with your location – town and state, and date
- Lead paragraph answering the five key questions —Who, What, Where, When and Why
- Main body of press release, around 2 more paragraphs, with additional quotes from you or any endorsement quotes etc.
- At the bottom of release; Contact Information—name, company name, phone, email address and website

Print Advertising

When you're struggling to gain editorial coverage, and desperate to get the marketing ball rolling and see your company featured in your favorite magazines, it can be tempting to throw some money at the problem and book some paid-for advertising slots.

Now, I'm not against print advertising, but—speaking as someone who spent literally thousands and thousands on ads over the first couple of years of my business—it's an area that should be approached with caution.

When my business first launched, I paid a designer to create some beautiful adverts and excitingly booked a series of ads in two leading women's glossy magazines that I felt were perfect for my target customer. Of course, the friendly advertising exec offered me such a great discount for a block booking that I signed up for 6 months worth of ads, saving myself 25% in the process. Total false economy! Within 2 months it became clear that the response rate to the ad was way off what I had hoped for, and the few extra sales generated didn't even come close to the cost of the ad, which even with discount was around $500 per issue, per magazine! Now that's not to say that the ads were a total loss—plenty of people had viewed them, and while the rush of customers and online orders I had hoped for didn't materialize, it definitely helped with my 'brand awareness' and at future craft and trade shows people were much more familiar with the brand. But it was an expensive lesson to learn.

One thing that also became quickly apparent was that whenever I gained any sort of editorial coverage, whether it was a feature about me and my business in a newspaper, or a product mention in a magazine, the response was significantly higher. I'd say around 10 to 20 times that of the response to an advert! Not only in customer visits to my website, but in actual sales too. It's been proven time and again that readers trust editorial content and connect more with an unbiased written feature or review than with an obvious sales ad. And it's free—all it will cost is your time!

Despite this, don't let my experiences put you off. If you want to, start small with a couple of well-placed ads in the right magazines for your target customer. Many smaller indie publications and zines offer much more affordable rates than the big fancy titles. It's difficult to gauge the success of a single ad, and sometimes it can take a few issues for readers to finally pay attention and respond to an ad, so negotiate a discount and commit to maybe 3 at first, and see how it goes. Whether you have a way to monitor traffic on your website, or notice a peak in sales, it will soon become apparent if an ad is working for you.

Start by drawing up a list of magazines that you think your target customer reads, and contact the advertising department and ask them for a media kit. They will then send you a nice glossy media kit, which will outline demographics for their readership, their upcoming issue themes (like, 'July Issue: *Red, White and Blue*,' so if you make a cool clutch bag out of vintage American flags, that could be a great issue for your ad, or even better some editorial coverage in the marketplace section!), and a rate card. Knowing the theme for each issue can also be a great way to focus your pitch to a features or marketplace editor, by choosing the right angle or products appropriate to that issue.

One thing to consider: you'll need a fantastic looking advert, who is going to design that? If you have the design skills, fantastic! If not, paying someone to design your ad is another cost to consider. And each magazine will have different size requirements, so it's not always a case of 'one ad fits all.' Be sure to include your logo and website URL. Chances are, you can only afford a small one, so it's important not to overcrowd your advert with too much information or too may words…have a look at similar sized ads in the magazine for ideas and comparisons.

Other PR Opportunities – TV And Radio

If you have an event coming up, this could be the perfect time to gain some valuable local TV or Radio coverage.

Call up your local Radio station and even the local, regional TV news program to find out the contact details for the Producer or Researcher for that show (don't just use the general email details that you may find on their website, you need to target the person who books the guests or researches the stories for that show). Email them a press release then follow it up with a call.

You can even try calling up a local radio quiz show—they always have a chat about what you do—as this gives a sneaky opportunity to get your info across. Don't forget to mention your website as it's the one thing people remember!

Think Local!

Using flyers and posters in your local area is a cheap and effective way to reach potential customers. It may take lots of leg work, but it can be worth the effort. Always keep a bundle in your bag as when you're 'off duty' and popping to the supermarket you may spot a gap in the noticeboard that's perfect for your flyer!

Deciding where to distribute your flyers is when you need to be as lateral in your thinking as possible. Think of places where people visit and spend time in your local area...some examples are:

Come Fly(er) With Me!!

Doctors surgery
Dentists surgery
Local playgroup venues
Libraries
Coffee shop noticeboards
Supermarket noticeboards
Tourist information centres

Gyms/health clubs/leisure centres/swimming pools
Yoga studios
Children's party, soft play and activity type venues
Veterinary surgery
Toy stores
Childrens clothes stores
Beauty salons/nail salons/spas/alternative therapy centers
Bookstores
Church hall noticeboards
Venues for girl scouts etc.
Food takeout places—waiting areas where people have time
to sit and notice flyers!

Local companies: Are there any large companies in your area? Why not pop into reception and ask if you can either leave some flyers there, or whether they have a staff 'intranet' or website that features ads or info? You could even offer a special staff discount code! Better still, they may allow you to hold a trunk show in their café or lobby area one lunchtime, a great chance to sell your products to a captive audience!

Local Events: Is there an annual 'Summer Fete,' carnival, fireworks display, funfair, thanksgiving parade or Xmas craft fair in your area? Or how about local school events? If so, these can be cheap and effective ways to promote your business—how about taking a stall, or simply handing out flyers. Rope in friends, family and kids too!

Marketing & P.R. Checklist

Have you done absolutely everything to market your business?

- Created a list of publications to target

- Requested a Media Kit from each title

- Reviewed each title and identified areas for your products or story

- Checked the masthead and compiled list of target journalists

- Checked the email address of each journalist

- Created a media database

- Emailed each journalist

- Followed up at least once

- Considered Local TV & Radio

- Created and ordered flyers for local distribution

- Started handing out flyers locally at every opportunity!

- Roped in family and friends to help distribute flyers too!

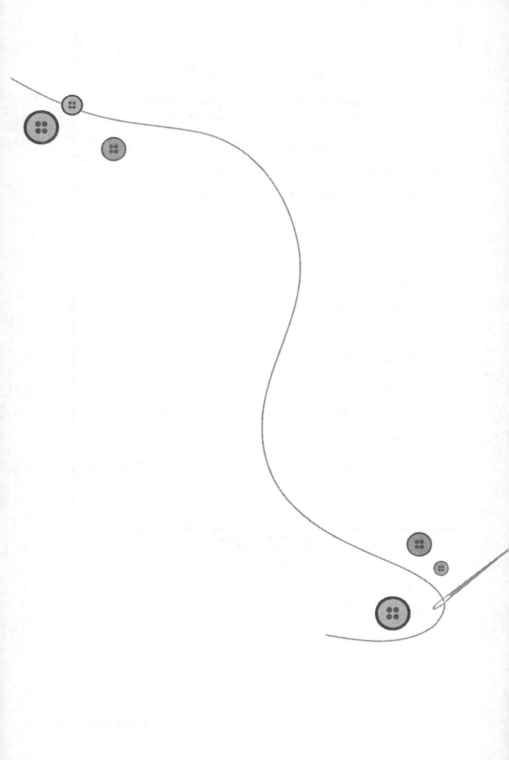

Chapter 6

Social Media & Online PR

Using Social Media for your Business

Word-of-mouth marketing has long been the most effective sales tool for businesses of all sizes. Why? Because we trust the recommendations of friends and family way more than any slick advert or glossy marketing brochure. When a friend says something is good—whether it's their mechanic, a local pizzeria, or a wonderful new jewelry designer's website—you trust their opinion!

These days, social media takes all the innate benefits of word-of-mouth marketing, and adds to it the capacity to reach thousands (or even millions) of people. Not only do we tend to share the same likes and interests as other members of our social networks, but we also tend to ask these people for advice on where to go, shop, eat, stay and play.

Developing a strong online presence is key to any new business these days—and the great news is it can be the cheapest and most effective form of marketing you will ever do. With just a little time and continued effort, using the likes of Facebook, Twitter, newsletters and even starting a blog can pay huge dividends. Here's how to get started!

Facebook

Facebook is not just for keeping tabs on friends and sharing your latest vacation snaps—it can also be used as a highly effective business tool. It's great for marketing your products and connecting with your customers. If you're just starting your social media marketing campaign—Facebook is most likely where you need to be. All you need is to create a 'Fan Page' for your business, and you're all set!

Creating a fan page is a straightforward process, but you do need to have the following things before you begin:

1) A Personal Facebook Account

"Why does Facebook require I set-up my business account through my PERSONAL account!"—this is one of the big questions I get from people who start the process of creating their business Fan Pages—and believe me, I also wondered this myself at first.

Think of your personal credentials as your 'badge' that you swipe every time you enter through the virtual gates of Facebook. Facebook's Terms of Service require that you use your real name & info—and your use of the features of the site (Fan Pages included) are dependent on your agreeing to abide by Facebook's rules & regs. Everything you create (photos, groups, Fan Pages,) are done by YOU, the real person. But, that does not mean that users of a business fan page will be able to access your personal info, be your friend, or even know it was you that created the page. Phew!

To sum it up—like it or not, you will need to have a personal profile in order to create a fan page for your business. I've heard of people creating 'fake' profiles in order to set up biz pages—but not only is this a violation of the TOS, but, it also robs you of the ability to quickly navigate between your personal profile & the administration of your fan page. Plus, chances are you're probably one of the 800 million people out there already signed up to Facebook anyway!

2) The Link to Create A Fan Page!
Why would Facebook make this one so darn difficult? True, if you log off of Facebook, you'll see the option to create a Fan Page for your business on the main login page, but assuming you're already logged in, you may struggle to find the option.

The first trick is to go to any page that you are already a fan ('liker') of and scroll down towards the bottom of the page while keeping an eye on the left column. By doing this you may eventually see a link to 'Create a Page.'

Want a short-cut? OK then. You've talked me into it! I'll share this super-secret link with you :

http://www.facebook.com/pages/create.php should take you to the 'create a page' page!

3) A Good Name
Hint: it is extremely difficult (bordering on impossible) to change your page name once you've made the decision. Other things can be changed fairly easily—but the name is here to stay.

For some businesses, this will be a breeze (the name of your business for instance), but take a second to think about your name, make sure you're spelling it correctly (seriously, this happens,) and do a quick search just to double check there isn't another FB group out there with the same, or very similar, name.

4) Branding & Other Info

The rest of the 'customization' of your Facebook Fan Page is fairly straightforward. While there are options for further customization (custom tabs) Facebook keeps a fairly standard look throughout the site & its many pages. Options you have for customization include: a profile image, info about your business, and the option to direct first-time visitors to a unique page.

Your profile picture will appear on the page (on the right column) and also as a thumbnail for all posts you make. In choosing your business page profile picture, I would encourage you to consider your overall branding efforts. If you have a logo—use it! You may have to modify it for FB purposes (to ensure it isn't cut-off in the thumbnail,) but you want to maintain consistent branding throughout all your social media efforts. Also, once you've selected a profile/thumbnail image, don't change it (or at least, change it VERY rarely!) Your logo will become visually associated with the content you're sharing in the newsfeed.

Your information is fairly straightforward. Be sure to include a web address when & where you can. Don't worry too much about things like 'hours' and 'parking'—even though Facebook may suggest you fill this info out (what fields you get depends upon which category you selected when you named your page.) At the end of the day, key information is WHAT you do, and (if applicable) WHERE you do it. Facebook doesn't give you much room to wax poetic.

In the 'Permissions' section of your page editing options, you can select what Facebook calls a 'default tab.' This is where your first-time visitors will be directed (all fans will be directed to the 'wall' view of your page). You can select: wall, info, photos, videos…and as you add different 'apps' to your page, you can add these too. This is how some pages achieve a more 'customized' look. A customized welcome tab can truly help set you apart, but you may want to focus on building an audience before you worry too much about more time-intensive design options (though you can pay a company to create a custom tab for you).

5) Fans…er, um…People who "Like" Your Business

Fan pages now have "likers" instead of fans. Once your business page is set up, you will need to have fans in order to have any impact at all.

I could go on & on about word-of-mouth marketing & the power of social media, but for right now we'll just say that fans are what makes your Facebook efforts worthwhile.

So, how do you generate them? Well...the first thing to keep in mind is that quality trumps quantity any day of the week. Focus on getting people that are truly interested in your product, service, or information. How do you do that? Here are a few helpful hints:

Take advantage of the "suggest to friends" option under your profile image (on the business page). This gives you the opportunity to share your page with your current (personal) FB friends. I mean, if friends and family don't support your endeavours, who will?

Integrate Facebook into your other web presences, like your website, Etsy store or blog. You can do this by using Facebook's own 'developer toolkit.' We recommend the 'like badge' and also integrating 'like' buttons. You can do this if you have access to HTML on your site (or know someone who does).

Mention your Facebook page in your other marketing materials. This means everything from email signatures, to email marketing campaigns, to business cards. Let people know!

Mention it in offline materials. For example, your business card, or customer postcards or comp slips could include: "Follow us on Facebook for specials offers, discounts and news."

And there you go! That's the basics of a creating a Facebook page for your business. I'd love you to "Like" my Facebook page: you can find me under 'The Craft Business Community!'

Twitter

Several years ago when I first heard about Twitter—a tool for instantly broadcasting the minutiae of your day and following the trifles of others— I couldn't imagine a bigger waste of time. Why would anyone care about what I had for lunch, or whether someone was headed off to the gym? Why would any business person want to get involved in such an obviously social platform?

Well, how wrong I was. Twitter is now used as a key business tool, and developing a Twitter following is now seen as a key part of any business marketing strategy.

How Does Twitter Work?

Twitter users—often called Tweeple (or worse)—have 140 characters to answer the question, "What are you doing?" If you join Twitter you can "follow" other tweeple, which causes their updates to appear on your home page. In turn, they can follow you. You can also direct message them, but always in 140 characters or less. Twitter communications can be viewed and updated on the Web, through desktop apps, and on mobile devices. In fact, such is the ease with which people can update and view their Twitter profile from their mobile phone, as a business-owner you have the ability to update and connect with your followers and customers literally in the palm of your hand!

How Does Twitter Help You Work?

Within this participating audience of exhibitionists are a growing number of people who are using Twitter for business. From large corporations to crafty entrepreneurs just like yourself, business owners in all corners of the globe are using Twitter as a communications and marketing tool.

Using Twitter for your business:

- Make sure your twitter name is the same as your facebook or business name so followers can make the connection easily

- The same goes for your profile image—use the same logo or image on all social networking sites and try not to change it—people will be used to the same icon appearing next to your posts

- Follow industry leaders who post links to important resources and influence conversations

- Post questions for quick answers and answer others' questions on anything crafty or business related

- Create links to your Web site or blog but (don't overdo it!)

- Keep up on the buzz in your industry—latest craft fairs or following what other crafters are up to

- Network with like-minded people

- Let your followers know about exciting new products, discounts, sales, craft fairs you're attending, or a great piece of press coverage

How to Get People to Follow You On Twitter

The more people who follow you on Twitter, the more influence and networking opportunities you have. Thus, it makes sense to try and build a following. Here are some ideas on getting others to follow you:

Follow them. There's an almost kneejerk reaction to follow people who follow you. However, there's a backlash against people who follow just about everyone for the sole purpose of gaining followers. In short, be discriminating with whom you follow. Align yourself with others in the same field as you: other crafty entrepreneurs or creative organizations like Craft Show companies or creative magazines, or simply crafty people whose work you admire.

Post some good tweets right before following someone else. I find that if someone follows me and they only tweet about how hungry or tired they are, I don't follow them back. The same goes for people who haven't tweeted in a while.

Complete your bio. People rarely follow strangers, so complete your one-line bio and include a URL in the More Info URL section of your profile. I can't tell you the number of times I've not bothered to follow someone because I didn't know a thing about them.

Add your Twitter feed to your blog or to other social media profiles.

If you have a following at your blog or a lot of connections at Facebook, you can leverage this audience to increase your followers at Twitter.

Reply to people you are following, especially if they're not yet following you. That's a good way to engage someone and get them to follow you, even if they didn't follow you immediately. Remember, though, some people have thousands of followers, and may not be able to respond to every reply.

For more ideas, or just to say hello, I would love you to follow me on Twitter @CraftyBiz. I promise not to tell you what I had for lunch.

Unless it was really good!!

Blogging

Like an online journal, a blog (short for web-log, by the way!) is a place to share your thoughts and knowledge on subjects related to your business, create links to useful information, and post news and other announcements. You can use a blog to give a personal face and voice to your business, and include interesting things that are going on in your life in general as well as the business, and create a useful resource your customers will want to revisit often. Blogs can also help you build your professional reputation and gain your customers' trust.

You can easily set up a blog for free, but they're not for everyone. Developing and updating your blog will require an investment of both time and thought, so before you get started, consider whether you can stick to a regular update schedule.

You'll want to update your blog at least once each week: keeping your content fresh will help show your readers that you're serious about your business. Your posts don't have to be long, but you'll want to keep them full of interesting news and comments.

Make a schedule for yourself, and dedicate time each week for brainstorming, researching article ideas, and writing your posts.

How Do I Start Blogging?

Well the great news is, starting your own blog doesn't even have to cost you a penny! There are tons of companies out there offering free easy to use build-your-own blog templates and, with just a little bit of effort and a smidgin of technical savvy, you could have your own beautiful blog up and running in just a few hours! If you already have a website for your business, your blog can be added to that, or have a link on the website to direct visitors to your blog.

Some of the best blog platform providers have so many useful tools to use, from widgets that you can place on your blog to link your readers right through to your Facebook or Twitter pages, to a Statistics bar that will allow you to check the traffic to your blog, where your readers are coming from and even what search words they used to find you. How cool is that?!

Blog Building Tools

www.wordpress.org

www.typepad.com

www.blogger.com

Branding Your Blog

Just like your website, the look and feel of your blog should reflect your personal and business style. Most of the blog templates available allow you to customize the design, adding in your logo or a banner and choosing the colors, layout and font that work best for you. Take some time to get this right as your blog really is an extension of your business. Think of it as another marketing tool and give it the same care and attention as you would if you were creating a flyer or brochure!

What Should I Write About?

The thought of sharing your hopes, dreams, plans and schemes with the world can be a little daunting at first: "What if I don't have anything interesting to say? What if I'm not funny/entertaining/witty/engaging? What on earth will I find to write about every day/week/month?"

The most important thing is to be yourself. If you're trying too hard to be something you're not, people can tell. Think of it as like being at a party where you don't know anyone. Yes, you do need to make some sort of an effort to be interesting and engaging and get to know people, but if you "try too hard" to be the life and soul of the party and that's not your natural character, then you'll just feel fake and a bit silly! If you speak honestly and from the heart, chances are what you have to say will be engaging and of interest to at least some people.

What you decide to share with your readers is entirely up to you. For some kinds of business blogs, maybe for more formal organizations, it may not be the best idea for the blogger to discuss their personal life; their readers may only be interested in the latest technical or financial information. But as a creative business owner, you and your business life are one and the same, and the kind of readers you attract are likely to also be creative individuals who are happy to share in your everyday trials and tribulations. You are a creative person who just happens to be running a business too. Now that doesn't mean posting daily blogs about your efforts to potty-train your 2 year old, but topics such as juggling your son's soccer game with getting ready for your first trade show, or moving home while trying to fulfill a huge pile of orders can give readers a cool insight into your work/life balance!

Photos

Photos are a key part of creating a visually interesting blog, and can be a great way to really promote your business too.

• Post photos of you at work in your studio, creating your latest range of products.

• Are you attending any events like craft fairs, trade shows etc? A perfect opportunity to share the journey and pics on your blog!

• Why not run a competition on your facebook, twitter, blog and website for previous customers to send in photos of them wearing/using your products. Offer a prize for the funniest/coolest pic. This gives you tons of great photos showing off your products in multiple settings!

• If you're an expert at making something in particular, an online tutorial can be a great way to find new fans and bring traffic to your blog and website. Check out You Tube for ideas from other crafty tutorials out there.

Email Newsletters

Email marketing is most effective when your subscribers request to hear from you. We've all had random newsletters from companies we've either never heard of or we once bought a product and ever since have been bombarded with daily special offers and ads. Very annoying isn't it?

I recently purchased a desk from an online furniture company, and now for the past few months, literally on a daily basis, my inbox has been filled with a stream of newsletters from this company. It drove me mad. An 'Unsubscribe' link was nowhere to be found on any newsletter, just small print directing me to their website to unsubscribe. On the website

I was then informed I had to write—snail mail, not even email!—to their head office to unsubscribe. To make it so very difficult for customers to unsubscribe from something they did not even request in the first place I think is terrible business practice and just plain sneaky, and left me mad as hell! One phone call and 2 very stroppy emails to their customer service department later and it's safe to say I won't be receiving any more newsletters from them ever again!! And it's also safe to say that it's unlikely that I will ever shop with them again either.

So always bear in mind that those on your mailing list should ONLY be those who have specifically requested to be kept up to date with your latest news and offers. While it may be tempting to copy over the entire contents of your address book, or ask friends or fellow crafty business-people for a list of their email contacts, this is a big no-no! Not only could this be against Data Protection laws, but it will reflect really badly on you and your brand.

Email Newsletters

So, the lesson with newsletters is to treat your customers/subscribers as you would like to be treated.

First up, only send newsletters to those who have actually requested to be added to your mailing list. This doesn't mean anyone who has ever emailed you or purchased something from you. They must have actively ticked or requested to be added to your mailing list.

Next, make it super easy for them to unsubscribe the minute they decide that actually, they'd really rather not receive any more info from your company.

Don't send too many, too regularly, or they will become annoying and lose their impact. Once a month is plenty, in my opinion!

Save newsletters for actual promotions and sales opportunities. You can use your twitter and facebook accounts to announce small, regular pieces of news. Save the email newsletter for a big sale or money off promotion that can actually drive people to your site to make a purchase!

Creating a Mailing list and Newsletter

There are tons of companies out there who can help you manage, create and send email newsletters. The best can offer the following features, all essential in creating great email newsletter campaigns:

Template builder: easy to use templates to brand and design a great looking newsletter that fits in with your company identity.

Opt-in form: this can be added into your website, blog, facebook page so that "fans" of yours can click to request being added to your mailing list. This info is then stored securely in your account to use for future newsletters.

Unsubscribe: each newsletter you send will also have an Unsubscribe' link to allow people to quickly and easily be removed from your mailing list.

Mailing list management: all the opting IN and OUT by your customers will be automated and your mailing lists updated instantly. You should also be able to view the number of new subscribers, and number of opt-outs too.

Payment: you can either pay for every newsletter you send (they charge per email address, so cost depends on size of your mailing list), or have a monthly unlimited plan.

Statistics: view how many people opened the newsletter, how many clicked through to your site, how many deleted without opening etc. An excellent way to gauge the impact of your newsletters – are they working for you?

A few Email Newsletter Providers:

www.verticalreponse.com

www.constantcontact.com

www.newzapp.co.uk

www.createsend.co.uk

The Final Word on Social Media Marketing

While all of the above may look like a ton of work, using social media to market your business could be the best thing you ever do.

When you compare the cost of just one print ad in a glossy magazine, or mailing out thousands of brochures or flyers, to what can be achieved and the amount of people you can reach using social media for FREE, you'll quickly realize that taking the time to set your business up for social media marketing could be the smartest thing you do for your business. So go on, get yourself out there and start (social) networking!

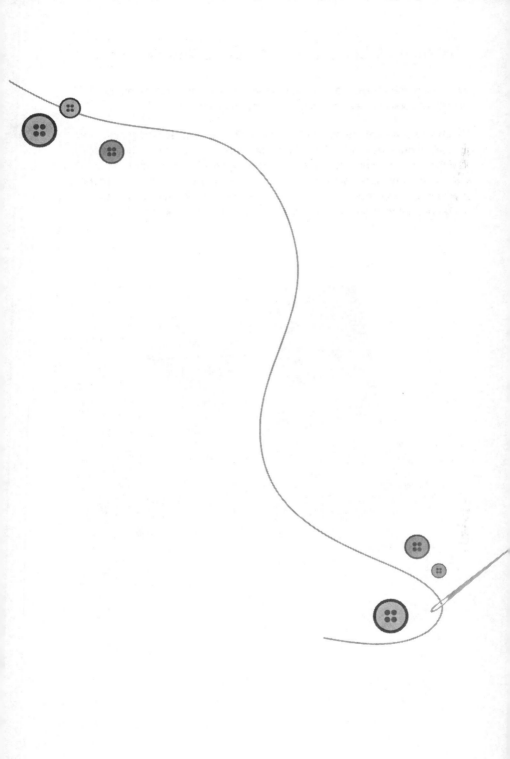

Chapter 7

Signed, Sealed, Delivered!

Sell, Sell, Sell!

As a crafty entrepreneur, there are so many ways to get your products into the hands of potential customers, and the more customers, the better, right?

These days, selling online is essential for any business, and with so many great resources available, setting up your online store is way easier than you may think. What's more, as well as having your own website, there are plenty of great online marketplace sites to choose from too. In fact, the hardest decision you may face is deciding on which is the best option for you.

Selling via Your Website and Online Store

Not so long ago, selling goods on your own website meant paying a web designer tons of cash to custom design a fancy website and build in an online store and shopping cart just for you. Nowadays, there are so many amazing online resources that, usually for just a small monthly fee, you can not only build but update, run and manage your very own website and online store yourself. Secure payment processing is all taken care of: customers can pay by credit card, debit card and Paypal and the money (less a transaction fee) goes straight into your account. These sites are so user-friendly that you don't need to be a tech geek to get to grips with them—if you can use a computer, chances are you'll be perfectly capable of using their great templates to get your own store up and running.

Most offer a large selection of templates to allow you to choose the style and layout of your store, and to customise it with your own branding, logos and colorways. Because you have the option to add additional pages (such as About, Contact Us, Returns, etc) you can also use these templates to create your entire website too. If you already have a great website, you can add this new online store part into easily.

Some of the better store-building sites now offer some great social media marketing tools as well, things like adding 'Like this on Facebook' icons, where customers can visit your store and tag their favorite items on their Facebook page, or you can post products, or special sale promotions, onto your Facebook fan page and link them directly to your store. There as so many great features available, it's a good idea to have a browse through the options of each supplier to see what works best for you.

Most sites also have tons of examples where you can click and view the online stores/sites of tons of other businesses who have used their tools—it's a great way to see what is possible using their resources!

Here are just a few of my favorites:

Online Store Building Sites

www.shopify.com

www.bigcartel.com

www.bigcommerce.com

www.ekmpowershop.com

www.moonfruit.com

www.volusion.com

Building Your Store

If you've already purchased your own domain name then your new store can be 'pointed' to that, so that all your marketing material will feature your website name and customers keying that in will go directly to your site/store. So, regardless of what company you use to build your online store, if people visit www.yourwebsite.com they can either automatically land on your online store or home page, or you can have a 'Visit' button on the main site that can link through to the online store.

Your online store should either match in with your existing web pages, or if you're building from scratch, you need to create a look and feel that is consistent with your 'brand' and all of your other marketing tools. The online site template you have chosen will provide you with details of what size and format your logo or 'banner' needs to be. This can either be created by you or your logo designer and inserted into your shop layout. You will then be able to choose the layout from a large selection of themes, and adjust the color and font of the display to create a website that looks a million dollars!

Here are some of the pages you will then create/add:

About Us

Pretty straightforward this one! This is just a small blurb telling your customers all about you, your company and your products. You can use this area to mention your company ethos, or mission statement, and more information about your products, how they are made, the materials or creative process involved. Basically the kind of information that will inspire customers to want to own one of your wonderful creations!

Policies / Terms & Conditions

This section should include details of how you intend to do business. If a customer is about to order something from you, this section should contain all they need to know about the ordering process:

- How much is Shipping? How will their goods be shipped?
- How long will it take to receive their order?
- What payment options are there?
- Do you accept custom orders, if so how do that work?
- What is the Returns Policy if they are unhappy with the goods for any reason?

Try to think of all the things a potential customer may ask, and aim to include them here.

When I launched my first online store, this part freaked me out. I didn't know what my Policies would or should be. I just wanted to sell stuff! I knew I wanted to offer great customer service, but I also wanted to be careful I didn't make any promises I couldn't deliver on! So I looked around at some of my favorite online stores and checked out the competition! What were their policies? How did they word the official stuff? How did they get this information across to customers without being too snotty or serious?

Contact Us

This should include your postal address (get yourself a PO box if you're not keen to have your home address out there!), contact phone number, email address for customer enquiries.

You may choose to offer several email contact options i.e. for Customer Enquiries email shop@yourcompany.com, for Press Enquiries it's press@yourcompany.com, wholesale enquiries to trade@yourcompany.com.

While it may be just you handling all these 'departments' for now, keeping the incoming email topics separate could make it easier to divide up tasks as your company grows!

You can also state your hours of business next to the phone number, so that customers are encouraged to call between, say 10am–5pm, and won't be surprised to reach voice-mail outside these hours.

Product Categories

Now that you've done the general info pages of your 'Store,' it's time to start adding your products! First up, jot down the various categories you need to cover. Say you made leather bags and accessories, these could include: *Bags, Satchels, Wallets, Keyfobs*. Then think of other ways your customer may wish to search i.e. *Women's Bags, Men's Bags, Women's wallets* etc. You can choose main category headings, then when the customer clicks on this they are presented with a sub-category to narrow their search.

Main Category: Leather Bags > Sub Categories: Womens Bags, Mens Bags

You can also allocate each product into several categories, so that it will show up in each relevant category. For instance, you may have a leather retro style satchel that you feel should be in both the women's bags and men's bags section, as well as in the Satchels category, so you can opt to include it in each category.

Obviously, you don't want to over-complicate things and make your customer jump through various hoops to find something, but choosing logical categories, and including the correct products in each, can make the browsing experience much simpler for your customers.

Product Photos

As discussed in Chapter 5, great product images are crucial—whether for your online store, sales brochure, or sending to magazines. Follow the tips in that chapter to create strong, clear images of each product, with close-ups and various angles to show each product in as much detail as possible. If your handmade cloaks have a beautiful silk lining, show it! If you're selling handmade bags or wallets, include a photo of the inside to show the interior pockets or lining. Give the customer as much visual information as possible.

Many online store templates will require you to upload your photos in a certain format (j-peg or gif file) and have a maximum size. So if you have very high resolution photos in a large file size, you may need to shrink them down for use on the online store.

The main 'thumbnail,' which will be the first image the customer sees of the product, should show the product in its entirety, clearly and with little or no background. Once the customer clicks through to the product description, you can then present them with a variety of other images. Make sure the color is a fair representation of the actual finished piece. Shadows or lighting can affect how a product's color looks in the photo, and if a customer is searching for a specific shade of yellow leather clutch to match their favorite dress, they would be most disappointed if a pale lemon clutch arrived in the mail!

Product Descriptions

This should be a clear and concise description of your product, giving the customer all the information they need to decide if this is the right item for them. Because a customer buying online can't touch, feel, smell or try on your product, it's important that they know enough from your Product Description to confidently go ahead and make that purchase. As well as an overall description, be sure to add more details like: dimensions, materials used, sizes available and care instructions (if your hand knitted cashmere throw is dry-clean only, it's important that they know that at this stage).

Size and Color Options

Your store template should also allow you at this stage to create drop down choices to allow you to list all the size and color options available. So your leather satchel may be available in Small, Medium or Large, and in the colors, Green, Teale, Raspberry and Plum, so you can provide all these options here. In the case of products with multiple size and color options, you would also consider a separate listing for each color, and then simply have a drop-down choice of Small, Medium or Large.

Price

Again, your template will show you where to add in the price for each item, and if you have price variations for each size or color you can add that in too.

Stock Control/Inventory

One of the great things about these online store templates is the information that only you, the store owner, can see behind the scenes. You can add in how many of each item you have available, and even create an "alert" when the stock of each item falls below a certain level.

Chances are, with a new, small business you'll quite easily know how much stock you have at any given time, but as your business and product lines grow, this can be a great way to keep tabs on your inventory.

Other stuff

Discount Codes: Having a Spring Sale and about to do a Newsletter offering your subscribers 20% off certain, or selected, goods, or 'Free Shipping' if they spend a certain amount? No problem, you can set up a Discount Code to give out to customers, and set the parameters like expiry date, what it can be used for and how many times, and in conjunction with any other discounts etc. Customers will enter this at the checkout to receive their discount. It can take a while to get the hang of using these extra features, and always make sure to test them out before doing a promotion.

The first ever Discount code I sent out was a disaster. I had made an error in the set-up process so instead of each customer only being able to use the code once, the code itself could only be used one time, period! So after the first person used it, all the other customers were shown an error message. Oops! And the newsletter had gone out to over a thousand potential customers (I had a great mailing list already due to running the sewing classes!)

A few stressed customer emails and a lot of fixing (and lost sales) later, and I fixed the problem. From then on, after setting up any discount codes, I made sure to visit my site as though I were a regular customer, and pretend to buy something using the discount code, to check if the discount was applied at the checkout. Only once I was totally sure that it was working correctly would I give it out to customers!

Other Features

Each online store template provider will vary, but here are more great features you can enjoy when building your online store.

Similar Items: "If you like this, you may also like these," shows similar items at the foot of the page of a particular product.

Customer communication: Click and generate "your order is being processed/has shipped" emails to your customers as you pack and ship each order.

Shipping Prices: Shipping can be calculated by product, by value, by country and various other methods. Research the true cost of shipping your products before you set your shipping prices, especially if your products are large or heavy!

Social Networking: Add "share/like" buttons next to each product, so customers can post on their facebook pages. Also buttons for your own Social Media: Subscribe/ Follow Us on Our Blog / Twitter/Facebook etc.

Sales Reports: Check your sales by date, product—see what are your busy months, which products are selling best, what impact each discount code has had.

Online Marketplace Sites

In addition to, or instead of, your own website and/or online store, there are many online marketplaces—many aimed specifically at handmade goods—where you can set up your own store-within-a-marketplace. This can be a great way to get started selling online, and many small businesses who already have a blog or website start with, say an Etsy store, and link directly to it from their main site. With these online marketplaces it's easy to join, and easy to leave if they're no longer working for you, so as your business grows you may opt to retain a presence on these marketplaces but also have your own main online store on your main website URL too.

Online Marketplace Sites

www.etsy.com

www.bonanza.com

www.folksy.com

www.madeit.com.au

www.notonthehighstreet.com

www.ebay.com

Service With A Smile!

One of the great joys of selling directly to the public can be the personal interaction with like-minded souls. Nothing is more rewarding than an email from a satisfied customer, or some great feedback left on your website praising your wonderful products or service. But, as the old saying goes "Happy customers tell 3 friends, unhappy ones tell 300," when the customer is less than satisfied it can feel like the worst thing that's ever happened.

Rule Number 1 is to treat the customer as you would like to be treated yourself.

If I emailed a vendor with a quick question about a handmade item and didn't receive a response for 3 or 4 days, not only would I assume that they're not going to be the most professional or efficient outfit around, but it may even make me question whether to go ahead and order from them. Will I ever get the goods? Will they be well made or well packaged? Or will I be chasing this person for weeks on end wondering where my goods are?

Communication is king! Always respond to your customers as quickly as possible, ideally within 24 hours. If you're going to be away for 4 days at a craft fair, set up an auto-reply stating that. Or better still, can you check your emails each evening after the show, or have them on your phone and send a quick reply when you can?

Keep the customer involved in each step of their order process and they will feel happy in the knowledge that their purchase is being dealt with. Confirm when an order has been received. Let them know when they can expect to receive their order. Inform them immediately of any delays, giving them the option to cancel if the delay means they no longer need the item.

Once the item has been received, consider a follow-up email checking if they are happy with their purchase, thanking them for their custom, and offering a discount on their next visit. You could even, on this email, invite them to subscribe to your newsletter or "join" you on Facebook.

Customer Communication Rules

Reply promptly, ideally within 24 hours, to ALL feedback

Treat the customer as you would like to be treated

Leave your emotions at home (or at least in the other room!)

Remain professional at all times

Communication is King!

Say Thank You!

Nice Touch!

The great thing about being a small business owner is that we have the freedom and flexibility to add the personal touches in our business dealings that large corporations can't. We can provide a genuinely human connection and create a pleasant experience for our customers, and add in those little touches that can make the experience more special for them.

It really is the little things that make a difference. Think about how you package and ship your orders. Could you use a cuter box, and wrap them in pretty tissue paper, sealed with a cool logo sticker? How about a handwritten note, wishing your customer lots of fun and enjoyment in using their new item? I have a pin-board full of cute business cards and postcards, with lovely messages that remind me of past gifts and purchases, and I often refer back to them and return to those online stores as I know that the owner genuinely appreciates my business.

I used to love including sweet little gifts when I shipped my craft kits— whether it was a pack of needles, handmade button fridge magnets, or a cute little vintage sewing kit and some stickers, my customers told me that these lovely little touches kept them coming back again and again.

So, have a think about how you can go that extra mile for your customers and make their day!

Return to Sender!

Handling Complaints and Returns

A couple of years ago I had a stressed-out mother of 3 calling because her large order of kids crafty kits had still not arrived, and Xmas was fast approaching. I had personally packed and shipped the order nearly 2 weeks before, and mailed it first class so it should definitely have reached her by then. As I hadn't paid extra for tracking, I had no means of locating the missing parcel. So I had a decision to make. Do I take the "sorry, not my problem, take it up with Royal Mail" approach, and leave her children without gifts? Or do I put the customer first. I quickly offered to re-send a whole new order, at my expense, recorded delivery to ensure it reached her on time. Now this little scenario cost me quite a bit in products and repeat shipping, and definitely wasn't something I could do on a regular basis, but to me it was worth it to gain a happy customer who was so delighted that she promised to spread the word amongst her friends. And I learned a valuable lesson—to pay that little bit extra to track larger orders in future!

Now, obviously your products are so wonderful and your customer service so dazzling that you'll probably never have to deal with such horrors, BUT, just in case, here's a few thoughts on dealing with the disappointed, the difficult and the downright dreadful!

In most cases, the customer will contact you directly to discuss their problem. Perhaps a piece is missing from a kit you have created, or the zipper on a wallet has jammed and they need a replacement. No problem – deal with them quickly and courteously, and send the replacement as quickly as possible, with a personal note apologizing for the hassle.

The Customer is Always Right...right?

Sometimes a customer, rather than contact you directly to discuss a problem or gripe, will decide to voice their unhappiness as feedback on your site, store, blog or fan page. Disaster! Now the whole world gets to see someone complaining about your products—does this mean your fledgling business is doomed? Now, we have no way of controlling if or when these things may happen, but we can control how we deal with these sorts of complaints.

Depending on where they have posted the comment, you could possibly delete the evidence and get on with your life, worrying as to whether they will crop up again, only this time even more disgruntled! Or you can tackle the problem immediately. Contact the customer directly, outside of the forum, and make amends—whether it's by offering a refund, replacement or otherwise. Deal with them promptly, professionally and apologetically and hopefully the matter can be resolved. Once that has been achieved, you can respond to their post, again apologising for the issue and repeating your offer to make things right, and how happy you are that they have accepted this method of resolution. That way, while your other customers can indeed see the negative feedback, they can see that you have been quick to deal with the customer and make amends. No matter how unreasonable or rude you may feel a customer is being, it's important to take the higher ground and not respond in an emotional or unprofessional manner—you'll only make yourself look bad and the customer even angrier!

You Can't Please All Of The People, All Of The Time!
On the odd occasion that I had any negative feedback or complaints from a customer, I would take it to heart and feel sick, worrying that my business was about to crumble and feeling terrible that someone else could be so annoyed at something I had caused. It took me a while to realize that, no matter how hard you work and how much you try to please customers, there will always be people out there that cannot be appeased. Deal with them graciously, refund their money, and move on.

Chapter 8

Show Me The Money!

Craft Fairs

So, your online store is up and running, you're on a roll with production and now it's time to meet your public! Selling directly to the public at craft fairs is the next logical step in your journey, and a key ingredient to really getting your products and presentation right before you make the leap into supplying to stores.

Selling your handmade products at craft fairs is not only a great way to make some much-needed cash, but it's also an excellent way of getting your name and brand out there, meeting like-minded crafters, and getting instant feedback from customers.

There's plenty to consider before you make the leap. These fairs can be pretty gruelling, take plenty of planning, a fair bit of cash, and you'll need to be prepared to work your socks off before, during and after. You'll be up at the crack of dawn, lugging boxes and setting up your table. Then spend all day on your feet, probably without so much as a toilet break, sometimes outdoors in unpredictable weather, praying that your lovingly handmade goods will sell like hot cakes.

But they can also be hugely rewarding, regardless of how many sales you make. Craft fairs are a great way to get instant feedback on your products, allowing you to develop your range and iron out any glitches before your business moves forward. They will also be excellent networking opportunities, not only can there be so much to learn from other booth holders, but you never know who you'll meet along the way!

So, take a deep breath, it's time to sell, sell, sell!

Finding the Right Craft Fairs

For your first fair, it may be a good idea to start with something local. This will save on travel and accommodation costs, and it will be far easier to rope in a friend or family member to help. Check the noticeboards in your local craft and art supplies stores for any adverts, search online, ask around in any online craft groups or forums, and speak to any other local crafters you may know. Some fairs may only run once or twice a year, so draw up a list of potential fairs and then it's time to research which ones may be right for you and your products.

If you're planning to do as many fairs as possible, in addition to local fairs, you may want to consider going farther afield. You will obviously incur additional travel and hotel expenses (unless you're lucky enough to have friends in other areas you can stay with), but if this allows you to sell at larger and busier fairs, it could be well worth the extra expenses.

Visit the websites of your favorite crafty businesses and see where they sell at. Don't be afraid to drop them a line, introduce yourself, and ask their advice on selling at a particular show. Their feedback could be priceless.

Once you've compiled a list of possible fairs for the next 12-18 months, it's time to do your research to see which ones are right for you.

• How long has the show been running for and how experienced are the organizers?

• How much is a booth or table, and what is included in that price?

• What sort of marketing efforts do they have planned to promote the show?

• What are the attendance figures for the show?

• How many vendors will there be, and what sort of products are being sold?

• Will your products fit in with the show—if the focus is heavy on art and ceramics, will your hand-stitched wallets be what visitors are looking for?

• Search on crafty blogs and forums and ask other crafters for feedback.

• Create a budget and calculate the total cost of attending that show, including booth, gas, hotel, meals and any staff costs. How much would you need to sell to cover those costs?

Once you've decided on your dream wish-list, it's time to apply to be a vendor.

The Application Process

Craft Fair organizers put huge amounts of time and effort into creating and launching their shows, then marketing and attracting visitors. It's important to them that they have the right mix of vendors and products to make the show interesting for visitors, and rewarding for vendors. Some may have a limit on the amount of vendors they have per genre. For instance, they may allow a maximum of 30 jewelry sellers, or 20 t-shirt people, and spread them throughout the venue, so everyone has a fair chance of selling their goods, and they don't end up with a show full of similar offerings. In addition to the type of goods you are selling, they'll be looking at the quality of your products and the style and branding of your company. They want vendors that can deliver interesting products, on a great looking booth, at prices that will attract customers.

They may ask you for website details, images of your products, marketing materials etc. It's important that you supply everything they ask for, in the exact format they ask for it, and in a professional manner.

If you're not accepted to a fair of your choice, don't give up. It's always worth asking for their feedback as to why you didn't make the cut. It could be that they are simply full as all previous vendors are returning and they give priority to existing customers. Or that they already have too many vendors in your genre. If this is the case, ask to be put on the waiting list, and stay in touch with them—check in regularly asking of any cancellations. If you show you're keen and persistent, you will be the first person that comes to mind when a cancellation arises.

If their responses are less clear, or they say they don't feel you are 'right' or 'ready' for their show—this could be polite code for "the information you sent us, or the product images or quality just didn't make the grade." Use this as an opportunity to take an objective view on your work and see where you could make improvements.

Once you've done your first couple of smaller, local shows, the bigger shows will be easier to gain access to, so stick with it and get a few local shows under your belt. And definitely attend the big show anyway, to get a better idea of how you can make the grade next year.

Fail To Prepare, Prepare To Fail!

If you're super organized and plan things carefully, you can avoid some of the trickier aspects of doing craft fairs and focus on enjoying the experience. There are so many things I wish I'd known before I did my first shows, so I'm really excited to share some tips with you, so you don't have to make the same mistakes I did!

Key things to check when booking a show:

- What size is my booth or table?
- Price and any hidden extras (tax, furniture, parking etc)
- What else is included? Do you need to bring your own chairs?
- If you need electrics or wi-fi are these available?
- Is there an ATM in the building? If not, be prepared to take credit cards!
- Is mobile phone reception good or problematic (I've done shows where there has been zero signal within the building, causing absolute chaos for vendors with wi-fi credit card terminals!)
- Do you need wall space to hang stuff? If you have a table, can you bring additional furniture or backdrops?
- If the fair is outdoors, is there a tent in case of rain? If not, can you bring your own awning?
- Is there vendor parking? How far away is it? How much does it cost? Do you need a permit?
- What is the procedure for loading in and out? How many hours in advance of the show opening can you enter to set up? How soon after closing can you exit the building?

Planning Your Booth or Table

By the time you arrive at the Craft Fair you should know exactly how your booth or table is going to be laid out, what goes where, and have all the displays and prices worked out so that you can set up quickly and easily.

You should do a full mock-up of your table a good couple of weeks before the show. Play around with how to display your items, making the best use of the limited space you have.

Use height to maximise the space – boxes hidden below fabric can create staggered platforms to display goods. An old coat rack, painted, can be a great way to hang lots of bags, hats, clothing etc. Ikea can be great for cheap shelving. Use cheap picture frames to display your price list or "Join Our Mailing List" type signs that will last from show to show.

Invest in a large vinyl banner with your logo that can be hung in front of the table at fairs.

It's vital your table or booth looks fabulous—look for inspiration online, (Check out the fantastic Flickr Group called Show me Your Booths: http://www.flickr.com/groups/715724@N24)

Planning for Your First Craft Fair

- Prepare a list of stock to make/take, and decide on prices.
- Prepare a price list and print off any signs.
- Make a Sales Policy/Returns info sign.
- Prepare price tags for each item.
- Make an Inventory list so that you can log sales as they happen.
- If you have a table, sew or make a tablecloth that covers it completely, as you will be storing stock beneath it.
- Make or buy a money belt, with several zippered pockets, for storing checks, notes and change.
- Prepare your 'cash float'—at least $100 in 10's, 5's and 1's, so you have enough change for your first sales.
- Get your *Show Kit Essentials* together: see end of this Chapter.
- If it's an outdoor show, you'll need suncream, sunglasses, a waterproof cover for both you and your table in case of rain.

Top Tips For Selling Success!

- Have items of various price points. If you sell $80 handmade leather bags, have cheaper items like wallets and even $3 keyfobs made from offcuts. Cheaper items will bring customers into your stand.

- Have special Show Exclusive Offers, like 2 for $20 or buy 2 bags, get a free wallet etc.

- Make sure all prices are clearly displayed—customers hate to ask, they'd rather know upfront what each item costs.

- Include sales tax in your prices.

- It's a sad fact of life that theft happens, even at craft fairs. Keep small items where you can easily see them, and big value items like rings should be secured to the display case with elastic.

- If possible, wear whatever you're selling, whether it's a t-shirt, necklace, beany hat etc.

- If appropriate, provide a mirror so customers can try items on.

- Have a mailing list sign-up sheet on a clipboard with pen attached. Encourage customers to leave their email address.

- Have plenty of flyers or postcards to give out, even to browsers.

- Have a receipt book handy, in case anyone needs a sales receipt.

- Relax, chat, sell, network, smile, have some candy in a bowl, start conversations, and enjoy yourself!

Loading In and Out of Fairs

One of the trickiest parts of doing a fair on your own can be the loading in and out process. Loading in is usually slightly easier as vendors may arrive at different times (especially if set-up is the day before the show opens), but loading out can be a nightmare for the unprepared!

Picture this—300 vendors, all tired after a long day, are desperate to load out and head home. There are only ten bays for cars/vans in the loading bay, so experienced vendors already have their husband/brother/best friend joining the car queue several hours before the show even closes. As soon as they show closes and they are allowed to pack up – bish, bash, bosh, they're all packed up, their friend is all parked up at the loading bay and arrives to help wheel the stock to the car. Eight boxes on two trolleys, and off they go.

On the other hand, you're all alone and couldn't wrangle anyone into helping you out. You can't leave your stand before the show closes—you're busy making sales. So you have to wait until the show closes. Pack up all your goods. Leave those goods all on their own while you head to the car park, collect your car, join the car queue and pray, pray that when you return to your booth or table hours later all your stuff is still there!

Not ideal, huh? Believe me, I've been there more times than I care to remember, so here's a few top tips:

• Invest in a collapsible trolley—my favorite one is called a Magna Cart, from Home Depot. It folds flat for the car, and can also be stashed on your booth or under the table.

• Where you park your vehicle may be some way from your booth or table. If you're using a trolley, pack your stock in same—sized boxes or plastic crates which can be stacked and wheeled easily on your trolley, 3 or 4 high, and also fit under your table—it's all about moving your stock in and out in as few journeys as possible!

• Think carefully about awkward items and shelving—can you realistically carry them alone?

- If the show runs across more than one day, on the night before the last day, thin down your stock. Remove large quantities of anything that's not selling well so that you will have enough for the final day's sales, but less to load out at the end.

- Keep your trolley and empty stock boxes under your table on the last day, not in the car. That way you can pack up everything the moment the show closes, then go and get your vehicle. By the time you have finished packing up, the car queue will have gone down!

- Get to know your neighbors—you'll need to ask them to keep an eye if you need to nip to the toilet or go collect your car. Often, others are in the same boat, so it's usual for vendors to form a bond and help each other out. I've made some great friends and contacts on the fair circuit!

Trade Shows and Wholesaling

Once you've been in business for a while and sold successfully online and on the craft fair circuit, you may feel ready to start wholesaling and selling your products into bricks and mortar stores. Before you book expensive trade shows and delve head-first into the crazy world of selling to national retailers, why not start by approaching some stores locally? This is a good way to grow your business at a steady pace, and will give you a chance to get used to dealing with retailers, figuring out how all the ordering, delivery and invoicing systems work, and get any glitches in your production systems smoothed out.

Credit Where It's Due

Getting your first orders from actual stores can be thrilling, and can make you feel like you're really on your way to becoming a proper "business". In an ideal world you would hand over the goods, they would hand you the cash, and everyone moves on (until they return, weeks later, with another big order and the same process repeats). In reality, the question of how to be paid, or how people will agree to pay you, can be a minefield. So you must decide at the outset what your sales and return policies and payment terms are, so that you can work with retailers efficiently and protect your company financially.

Terms

Retailers will often ask for your 'terms'—this refers to how you expect to be paid for the goods that you will supply to them.

C.O.D: Cash On Delivery. 3 words: **Don't. Do. It.** In this day and age, it's neither wise not necessary to engage in the hassle and uncertainty of shipping goods and praying the order is accepted and a check issued forthwith. For new customers, it's Pro Forma all the way.

Pro Forma: This is where you will require payment, usually by credit card but can be by check or bankers draft, in advance of goods being delivered. You take a retailer's credit card details when they place the order, and only charge their credit card on the day you ship their goods. Until you have established a good working relationship (and credit checked) new customers, all orders should be Pro Forma.

30 Days Net: These days this is the standard for most small to medium retailers. Once you ship the goods you invoice them and can expect payment 30 days from the date of invoice or date they receive the goods, depending on their procedures.

60 Days Net: If you're lucky enough to have orders placed by some of the larger, national retailers, well done. But on the flip side, these larger chains are often the ones to dictate the terms and you must accept their payment schedule, which can often be 60 or even 90 days net. Given that you have to buy supplies, make then ship the goods and then wait a further 60- 90 days to see any payment, this can cause a major cash-flow headache for the small supplier. So before you agree to any big orders, it's important to figure out of you can realistically afford to fulfill that order and wait for payment.

Consignment: This is where, rather than purchasing goods and paying you for them outright, a store agrees to display your products and sell them on your behalf, then you each take an agreed share of the sale price. This is most common in smaller shops and galleries who perhaps lack the cash-flow to place big orders, but who wish to support local artisans and offer a wide selection of handmade items.

A consignment split can be anything from 50/50 to 30/70, though 40/60 seems to be the most common (40% to them, 60% to you). It's up to you to haggle and agree on a mutually satisfactory split. Remember, while they may not be paying you money for your goods up front, the store owner still has all the usual overheads—rent, rates, insurance, utilities, staff, credit card fees and so on, so they need to make a decent margin too.

When you're just starting out, placing stock on consignment in a few hand-picked stores can be a good way to get your products out there. I would advise only to do this with stores close enough to home that you can deliver product/collect payment in person. This way you can check up on how your goods are being displayed, have a chat about what's working and what's not, and build a good working relationship with the store owner.

Make sure you're clear, and have in writing, the terms of your agreement. How regularly, and by what method payments will be made to you, whether any damaged or stolen stock is the responsibility of you (most likely) or the store owner. Ask them for details of other crafters who they also stock on consignment, and contact them for a reference and any feedback. Any decent store owner will be happy to provide this kind of information.

Wholesaling Policies

Returns Policy: When your sell your goods wholesale to a retailer, it's on the understanding that the goods are purchased outright. Unless a customer really demands an adjustment to your returns policy—say they want to take a certain amount of stock but have the option to return any goods unsold within a certain time period if they're not selling—just say no to returns. The hassle and expense of having goods returned—who will pay for the return shipping, what if some goods are damaged etc., means it's just not worth it. If you really, really want to have your goods in a certain store, and the retailer demands you accept returns, make sure you are both clear on the agreed terms and put them in writing.

Minimums: Order minimums can relate to the amount of each line item that needs to be purchased, and the minimum of the total order value you will accept. If you set no minimums, then a store ordering 1 each of 5 items isn't exactly wholesale is it? Really they're just buying 5 items at half of the retail price!

For smaller value items in particular, like a greetings card or key-chain, you may wish to set a minimum order of 6 units of each style, and this should be reflected in your Line Sheet.

It's also a good idea to set a minimum order quantity. This needs to be low enough that smaller stores can take a few of each item to try out your products without having to commit to a huge financial outlay, but high enough that it's worth the time spent on the packing and admin that each order entails. Your minimum order value could be as low as $100 or as high as $2000, and much will depend on the retail value of your products. If in doubt, start fairly low to get some retailers on board, then review.

Shipping and Lead Times: When retailers place an order, especially for hand-made items, they usually expect to be given a date in the not too distant future for delivery. Some may request a date several months away: they're planning way ahead for their Xmas stock. Others may ask for stock asap. Balance the requirements of the retailer with your ability to product the goods for that order, and once you agree a date with them stick to it. Think carefully though—if you agree to shipping 200 handmade leather wallets in 10 days, then you're gonna be pretty busy!

It's common for retailers to expect free shipping if they place an order over a certain value—most companies offer this as an incentive for retailers to place a decent sized order. So you may have an order minimum of $100 and offer Free Shipping for order over $250. Bear in mind that the cost of shipping is now coming out of your profit margins, so think about this carefully.

Resale tax Form: Whenever someone makes a wholesale purchase from you, you will need to get a copy of their reseller's permit number for tax purposes. You should incorporate this into your order form, so all of their information is in one place.

Line Sheets / Order Forms

Creating a Line Sheet

A Line Sheet is a form that lists all of your available products, and their wholesale and suggested retail prices, and minimums. A line sheet can also be used for taking orders, and should be something a buyer can take away with them to fill in their order requirements and fax back to you.

It should include:

- Your company letterhead, logo and contact information, including your email address and phone and fax numbers.

- Area for the buyer to fill in their information: Company Name, address, phone, fax and email, Contact person at company.

- The Bill–To address and the Ship-To address (as these may differ).

- Credit card information: type of card, number, expiry date, security code.

- Resellers Tax Permit Number.

- A line-by-line listing of each of your products. You will need to assign an Item Number to each item. For instance, if you have Sock Monkeys in 3 colors you could allocate SM1, SM2 and SM3 to these. You should include a short description of each item i.e., Sock Monkey—Green.

- Columns for Minimum, wholesale price per unit, sub total.

- A place for the buyer to sign and date.

Get hold of a couple of order forms from similar businesses to yours and see how they lay theirs out!

Trade Show Secrets!

Lots of people exaggerate how many orders they have taken. Don't worry if your neighboring booth holders tell you how well they're doing, yet you've only taken a few orders. Don't feel like a loser in comparison— chances are they're just 'bigging it up.' Don't' fall into this trap yourself and reveal too much, a simple "it's going great!" will do!

Show management can have a terrible habit of exaggerating the success of a show. Often on the last day of the show they will walk the floors, meeting and greeting the exhibitors, telling them that this particular show has had record-breaking attendance and has been a huge success. In reality, the show may have been deathly quiet, with many vendors complaining of a lack of orders. So take such stories with a pinch of salt and judge for yourself!

Some trade shows have a rigorous application process and claim to have waiting lists of several years—tactics that are sure to make you want to show their even more! In reality, yes the show may be incredibly popular, but often this is their way of weeding out the weaker companies that they'd rather not grace their floor space! All good exhibitors need a mix of new and established brands and products to keep the buyers coming back, so If you have a product that is hot and new, they will find a place for you, regardless of 'waiting lists'!

Some people will go to trade shows purely to steal other designer's ideas. The more trade shows you do, the more you will be able to spot them easily. These people will hover, rarely engage in conversation, and try to wait until you are busy with another customer then quickly grab your marketing materials and leave. For this, and other reasons, most booth holders keep their product brochures behind the counter and only hand them over after a chat with a buyer and receiving their business card. Any decent buyer will attend these shows armed with plenty of cards as this is pretty standard.

Buyers from big retailers often flip their badges over so that it's not immediately obvious who they are. I guess it allows them to browse without being jumped upon by every excited vendor whose booths they enter. But, if you spot a flipped badge, don't assume that your big Nordstrom's order is minutes away—competitors, journalists and all sorts of other people can do this too, so if you see a flipped badge, have a chat. Introduce yourself. Find out who they are!

Location, Location, Location

When booking your space at a trade show, or any show for that matter, don't just take the first booth space offered to you. Ask to see a floor plan and print it out. Call the exhibitor to go through all the booths available in your price/size range and highlight them on your floor plan.

A good location is in a high-traffic area near entrance doors, escalators, elevators or washrooms. A bad location could be in a far corner, or on the outside wall opposite a large bank of unused doors. Once you've narrowed down the available booths in your desired size, you may also want to be close to or opposite a big, established brand that will be bringing plenty of traffic to the area. Ask them who is nearby, and discuss with them which booth should get the best footfall.

Often, exhibitors will charge more for a corner spot—depending on your booth layout this could work well for you as your booth will be open on 2 sides, capturing visitors as they come down 2 different aisles. On the other hand, if your products require wall space to hang and display them, being in the middle of a run of booths will give you wall space on 3 sides.

The difference between a good and a bad location could turn out to be huge in terms of orders, so it's worth taking the time and asking the right questions to get the best possible location.

Trade Show Do's and Don'ts

Do wear comfortable shoes: you'll be on your feet for several days so it's important that you are comfortable.

Don't go into a direct competitor's booth—you wouldn't want them in yours! I once had 2 women who ran a rival company to mine, selling very similar kits, visit my booth pretending to be retailers, purely so they could get their hands on my new catalogue and product details. Sneaky, but it happens all the time!

No matter how quiet it may be at the end of each day, **never**, ever leave your booth early. Exhibition rules state that you must remain at your booth until the hall has cleared and, besides, you never know which buyer may be planning on stopping by on the way out.

Don't eat in your booth in front of customers. This can be a tricky one when you're manning the booth alone, but if it's absolutely vital, be discreet and choose your lunch wisely! I always have a big breakfast, just in case I don't get the chance to eat for the rest of the day.

Keep a stash of mints and a bottle of water handy so you can stay fresh and chat confidently all day long!

Don't sit down unless you have a good medical reason! You should always be standing, ready to engage with visitors.

Don't take marketing material, or photos, of any other exhibitor's booths without their permission. It's just not cool!

Stay positive. It's easy to get bogged down in a massive moan-fest with your fellow exhibitor's, especially on a slow day with few buyers in sight. Keep a smile on your face and your positive energy will shine through!

Never, ever, take a book! Sure, trade shows can be 3 or 4 long, grueling days and it's tempting to sit down with a coffee and a read when the day slows down. But this gives the impression "Hey, she's not busy at all, her products can't be that popular!"

However, appearing 'busy yet available to chat' can also put browsers at ease, so if there's something you could be doing— say stapling together more press packs, or making something small that relates to your handmade products—that could also be a good idea. As long as you have the space and can easily stop what you're doing the moment you're needed.

Look busy, stay positive, network, watch and learn!

Countdown to Your First Trade Show!

12 Months To Go: If you're just getting started with your new business right now, chances are it will be at least a year before you'll be ready to do a trade show, so start thinking now and you could be visiting this year with a view to exhibiting next year! If you can, narrow it down to shows you feel might be right for your products, and attend the show as a visitor the previous year to get a feel for the show. Walk the aisles, absorb as much as you can—look at booth design, the best locations, hot products, and if they're not busy with buyers, have a chat with other exhibitors. I found this invaluable and got some fantastic advice, and genuine feedback that really helped me decide which show was right for me. Also, the relevant trade publications in the industry will have a presence at these shows, grab yourself a free copy as you will be approaching these very magazines about your own products very soon!

6 Months To Go: Start talking to show staff about becoming an exhibitor. The best booths will go quickly, so you will need to decide and book yours way up front. Staff will be starting to put together the Directory for the show, and as a 'hot new exhibitor' you could grab yourself some free editorial. These directories go out to thousands of buyers in advance of the show, and they use this to plan their day, so a great feature on your new product with a "Find Us at Booth D24" could be an amazing coup!

I got myself coverage like this on several occasions and it worked wonders—buyers who had read the magazine and liked my products had actively sought my booth out at the show to place an order. Invaluable!

3 Months To Go: Check the exhibitor's manual to make sure you meet all the important deadlines for booking electricals, lighting, furniture and any extras on your booth. Get your travel and accommodation organized—most big shows have deals with travel agents and special exhibitor's rates in local hotels.

2 Months To Go: Decide on your booth design. This is the most important thing you can do, so get it right. If you have the space, set up a mock-up of your entire booth in the garage or spare room. Double and treble check the dimensions and materials used for your booth.

1 Month To Go: Make sure all your product brochures, press kits and line sheets are ready. If you haven't done so yet, change your email signature to feature "Come See Us At XYZ Gift Fair on this date, Booth D24." Email any buyer whose details you have with a brief hello, description of your products, and how you hope to see them at the show. Include your booth number.

2 Weeks To Go: Ship any goods. Decide on a 'smart yet comfortable' outfit for each day of the show. Have a run through with any staff or people who will be assisting you on your booth. Send out press kits (see below) to any journalists covering the show.

My Trade Show Disaster Story!

I made a huge mistake once—having already done several big trade shows where the booth walls were the standard grey felt wall panels, I had created a booth design that used Velcro hook'n'loop on the rear of custom made posters, so that the entire booth walls were covered. This was a great cost effective way of decorating and branding my booth, as it was super quick to put up, and the laminated posters could be used again and again.

I then rocked up to a new trade show, only to discover that this particular exhibitor built their booth walls from hardboard, painted white. My Velcro posters were no use here! Not only that, the dimensions were slightly smaller than expected. I was alone, and freaking out. Fortunately, in my trusty Show Kit, I had all I needed—craft knife, scissors, pins, nails, hammer, double sided tape etc to find a way to attach my display posters to the new background. But, let's just say I never made that mistake again!

Getting The Most Out Of A Trade Show!

Get together your press kit and check the exhibitor manual—or ask the exhibitor—for a list of all the journalists who will be covering the show. Send each journalist a press kit, a sample of your product, and your booth number with a short "come see us!" note. Journalists are actively looking for hot new stories to write about from the show, so this pro-active approach can work wonders.

Take 10 additional press kits to the show. Every decent show will have a press room exclusively for journalists where exhibitors are encouraged to leave press kits for them to choose from. Make sure you leave them there the day before the show opens—after you've finished setting up your booth perhaps.

Consider advertising in the Show Directory. These are mailed to tens of thousands of buyers, not all of whom can attend the show, and many use this as a research tool to find hot, new products. If you've managed to gain some editorial coverage, try to have your ad placed on the opposite page or nearby if possible. It's worth hiring a graphic designer to create a really slick ad for this.

Take plenty of business cards. Not all the contacts you make will be buyers, so a business card with your personal contact details beats handing out an expensive brochure to all and sundry!

Be friendly and chat to as many other booth holders as possible. Everything I learned about trade shows, I did *at* the show, not beforehand! More experienced vendors will have a wealth of advice and tips. Listen and learn, then pass it on to the newbies next year!

What's In a Press Kit?

You don't have to spend a fortune on creating your press it, but it does have to be eye-catching, professional looking and stand out from the crowd. Your press kit could be the one chance you have to make a great first impression!

Presentation Cover: This will hold all the contents together and be the first thing people see, so make it unique and stand out from the rows and rows of other press packs on display. Maybe you could **use the** recycled cardboard and bright red ribbon that is featured in your packaging...or attach a beautiful beaded bag charm from your range to catch their eye. Packs in bags always work well but lots of companies are doing this now. Still, a canvas tote bag with your company logo or cool phrase printed on, and press kit inside, could be a great investment!

Press Release on letterhead: If you have an interesting background (i.e. "founded by ex- masseur to the stars Lara Smith, the Star Balm range of body and massage oils are mixed by hand in South Carolina..."). Journalists love an entrepreneur with an interesting back-story.

Company Biog on Letterhead: Make this no more than one page, outlining who you are, what the company is about, your mission statement, and who your customers are.

Product Brochure: Include your price list/line sheet so journalists can see the price of each item.

Press Clippings: If you've gained any press at this point, include color copies in your press kit.

Booth Number: Make this as prominent as possible—on your presentation cover or bag, again on the press release, anywhere you can. Journalists need to be able to see it and find you easily.

Show Kit Essentials!

Scissors

Tape, sticky dots, double sided tape

Stapler

Craft Knife

Staple Gun

Glue gun

Bulldog clips, rope or twine

Pins, nails, hammer

Lots of pens – they always go awol!

"Back in 2 Mins" sign

Sheeting or fabric to close off your booth each evening,
or over stock in event of rain/toilet break!

Calculator

Several clipboards – for writing up mailing list, order forms

Business cards

Garbage bags

For you:

Breath mints, Tissues, Fresh wipes, Lip balm/lipstick,
snacks, coffee flask, bottles of water

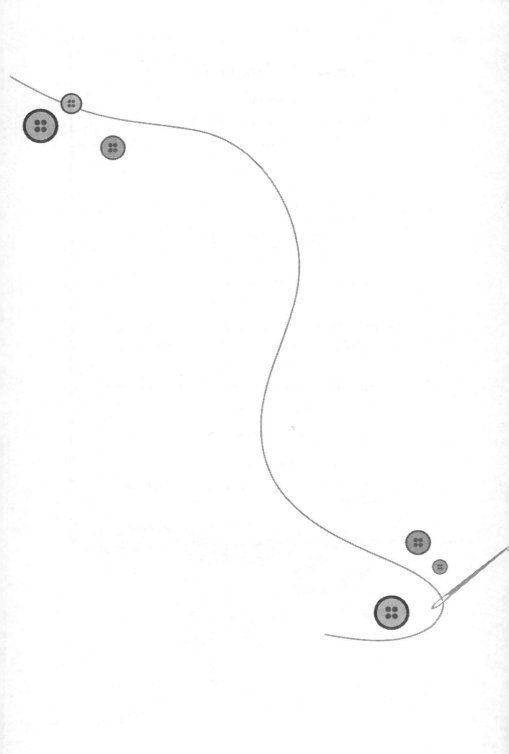

Chapter 9

The Next Steps

HELP
WANTED!

Review and Reflect

When you're self-employed, it can be all too easy to get caught up in the day to day demands and deadlines that running a small business demands, and lose sight of your original goals. It's important to take stock every so often—whether it's every 6 months or every year—and think about what you have achieved so far, and where you hope to take things from here.

You may find that your business could now look very different to how you originally imagined. Is that a good thing or a bad thing?

Maybe the business has grown so much quicker than you could even have dreamed, and you feel as if you're being dragged along on a runaway train, fighting to stay in control? So many great opportunities have come your way, that you're battling to stay on top of things and wondering how on earth you're going to continue to cope. You need more space, more help, more time, more knowledge, but you're so busy fire-fighting on a day-to-day basis that you simply don't have the time or the energy to plan the next phase of development.

Or perhaps things have been much more of a slog than you had anticipated. The orders you hoped for just haven't materialized, and you're struggling to pay the bills and retain the enthusiasm you had in the beginning. You're not sure if you really want to continue.

Call It Quits, or Push On Through?

Whatever challenges you are facing in your business, rest assured that for every problem there is a solution, and what you are currently going through has been experienced by thousands of entrepreneurs before you. You will get through this. If you want to, that is.

But, most importantly—business situation aside—how are *YOU* feeling?

Are you happy? Is running your own business what you expected? Are you enjoying the majority of the process, or have you come to dread each day? Turning a hobby into a career can be hugely challenging, and there's no shame in admitting that actually, this may not be for you after all. Sure, you may feel embarrassed admitting to all the friends and family who have so eagerly supported you that, actually, this just isn't working out for you.

Before you walk away, let's troubleshoot and look at some of the most common reasons for *Crafty Business Fatigue*. What changes need to occur for you to have more fun and make more money, and what steps do you need to take to implement these changes?

Problem	Possible Solution
Loneliness: you miss the day-to-day interaction with other people	Hire some shared space in an artist collective or creative studio environment. Or hire some part-time help at home.
Running out of space at home	Consider a storage unit to store the bulk of your stock and materials. Look for an affordable studio space. Or use fulfillment house so you no longer keep large amounts of stock.
Bored of making large amounts of the same product	Consider employing help ith making your products, or outsourcing certain parts (like cutting all the fabrics, or packaging up kits etc).You can still retain quality control while delegating the simpler tasks.
Large orders and way too many products to make	As above, but outsourcing production completely. You could start off employing local moms who work from home. Or if you have space, part-timers who come to you.
Bogged down with day to day admin tasks.	Hire a bookkeeper, virtual PA or part time help to assist you with invoicing, packing and shipping goods, boxing up products etc.
Swamped with orders, spending too much time packing goods	Consider using a fulfillment house to store and ship your product.
You don't enjoy selling, or need to find more stockists for your products	Find the right Sales Rep who will get your products into stores.
You're working way too many hours a day and have lost all sense of work/life balance.	Read on to the end of this Chapter, and consider all of the above options so that you're working *smarter*, not *harder*!

If Working From Home Just Ain't Working Any More!

When your spare room or garage is bursting at the seams, and your business seems to have taken over every aspect of your life, physically and mentally, it's so tempting to dream of hiring a space dedicated to your business. Moving from home to your own studio is a huge leap and it's important to get the timing right.

Move, or Improve?

Lack of space—unlike many other home workers who can get by with a laptop, some files, and a small office area in the corner of a room, being a crafty entrepreneur usually involves a ton of STUFF! And the sheer amount of stuff can quickly grow, to the point where you're tripping over packaging in the hallway, stacking supplies in the bedroom and hogging the dining table with your makeshift production lines! Believe me, I've been there!

Could you hire a storage unit nearby to hold bulky stock and only keep the essentials at home? I started with this method, and visited my storage unit a couple of times a week to pick up materials, drop off completed kits, and pack and ship orders. Yes, it was slightly inconvenient, and at times I dreaded the trips, but it was way cheaper than hiring a studio, and it bought me precious time working from home while the business grew to a point where it could realistically afford a dedicated space.

Can you afford it? The great thing about working from home is that it's pretty much free. When a business is starting out, it's vital to keep your overheads low. So while you would love a nice, airy studio, can you really afford it and do you want the worry of having to make the rent each month?

Will you miss the convenience? As you take that leisurely stroll from bathroom to home office, or pop some laundry in the dryer while you wait for someone to return your call, think about what you may miss if you no longer worked from home. Sure, you're excited about separating work and home life, and desperate for your home to return to being just a home, but sometimes the grass isn't always greener. Getting business premises means commuting, being away from the house all day every day, and losing all the perks that home working can offer. Are you ready for that?

It's Lonely at the Top (And the Bottom, and Middle!)

One of those pitfalls of working for yourself is the isolation factor, also known as Cabin Fever! Working at home, alone, isolated from the world, in the same place can slowly but surely drive a person round the bend. Impossible as it may sound, you might even find yourself starting to miss those annoying colleagues and that irritating boss!

It's easy to assume that hiring a studio space will provide the solution to the problem—but the money spent on rent could be used to hire extra help…which would provide an extra pair of hands AND the company you are missing. Otherwise you may find yourself working alone in a lovely studio space, and feeling just as isolated! That happened to me, and ironically, after months of dreaming of my lovely new studio space, I found I soon missed the comforts of working from home. Typical!

Fortunately, there are some things you can do if you feel isolated and a little bit lonely. One of those things is to make sure you leave the house every day, regardless of how busy you feel, or how cold, wet or windy it may be outside!

Even though the majority of a crafty business people's work probably requires them to be in one place with all their materials to hand—making or packing their products—you could set aside a certain time each afternoon for answering and sending emails, keeping on top of your blog and social networking. And that can be done from just about anywhere, if you have a laptop. Take a walk in the fresh air to your favorite café, pitch up for even half an hour to an hour to do your online work whilst enjoying a well-earned latte, then stroll home again—even just an hour away from the workplace can give you that boost you need to get through the rest of the day and stop you from going stir crazy! Something as simple as going for a walk just to get a breath of fresh air can take away that sensation of the walls closing in around you.

If you've considered all of the above, but feel that it's really time to move on and move out, consider the following:

- Is the company earning enough to pay rent? How much can you afford?
- Don't run before you can walk—you may be on a high from a couple of big orders and feel the time has come to trade up. Can you be 100% sure that the business will continue at this rate?
- Are you able to make a long-term commitment (you may need to sign a lease anywhere from 24–48 months)?

- Are you happy to share a space, or do you require a place of your own?
- Do you know any other fellow crafters in a similar position that you could go in with?
- Put the word out that you're looking—ask around your local craft stores or at your next local craft fair, email everyone you know, and search online for low cost creative work spaces. There are subsidized artist studios and workspaces in most major cities that you may be eligible for.

Outsourcing and Hiring Help

Outsourcing Production

The aim of any business owner is of course to sell more products. More sales equals more profit, equals business success! But the irony of being a crafty entrepreneur is that actually, more orders can sometimes mean a major headache, as eventually you reach a point where you cannot physically make any more items yourself than you are already doing (and you're no doubt working round the clock already just to keep on top of things).

So unless you want to work yourself into an early grave, the only way to move forward with your business is to find a way to produce more goods, while retaining the same quality that your reputation is built on. It's time to either hire help or outsource production completely.

Most crafty entrepreneurs I know, myself included, experience a mid-point between trying to do it all themselves and outsourcing production completely. When my range of craft kits really took off I received a large order form a national department store chain. With all the other demands of trying to grow my business, I knew that there was just no way I could make over 1000 kits in just a couple of weeks. (I had three months between receiving the order and actually delivering the kits, but because I had to order all the materials up front and pay my own suppliers within 30 days, then wait 90 days for the company to actually pay me, I needed to order my kit components as late as I possibly could, so that the gap between paying for all the components, and receiving funds from the store was as short as possible!)

So I asked around and found that several friends knew stay at home moms looking for part-time work. Two of them were free to come to my house several days a week (we did it in shifts, there was only one kitchen table!) and another was happy to cut fabric and bag up small components like buttons and needles from home. And so my rather hotch-potch first big production run came together.

Growing like this was great for me for a couple of reasons. I was able to use my part-timers as and when I needed them, and because they were not officially full-time employees, I paid them an agreed hourly rate on the understanding that they were self-employed individuals and responsible for their own taxes and reporting. So I was able to get help when I needed it without the commitment and expense and hassle of taking on a permanent member of staff.

Also, having made all the kits myself before then, all the information was in my head (along with everything else—it was pretty crowded in there!). Working with others forced me to transfer all the info from my head into actual transferable information—together we created a 'cheat sheet' for each kit style—a guide to the contents of each kit, measurements of each fabric, which patterns were included etc. After a few months of working alongside the girls making kits, I felt confident enough that I could leave them to it and, with their experience of working with me together with the invaluable 'cheat sheet,' each kit would be made with the same quality control as if I had created them with my own fair hands!

Using a Sales Rep

Once you have your production sorted, you've done a few trade shows and you're already wholesaling to plenty of independent stores, you may feel it's time to up the ante and find yourself a great sales rep who can get your products into lots more stores. An independent sales representative or sales representative organization (or group) will offer your products to their established gift buyers who are ready to buy new items for their stores.

Sales reps' main purpose is to introduce, educate and take orders for product lines and they receive a commission as compensation. Reps commissions are taken out of the wholesale price of the product rather than on the price differential between buying and selling prices. Using sales reps can often be the best and most cost-effective way for companies interested in expanding sales regionally or nationally.

Hiring a rep can be one of the best ways to grown your company in the wholesale market arena. Connecting with the right rep is often as easy as just talking to the right people.

Store buyer referrals are an excellent source of information regarding good sales reps. Visit with the owner/manager of your local gift store and ask them to share with you what companies have good sales representation that may be looking for new products.

Talk to other producers in your niche who have successful sales reps. Most established gift manufacturers or producers can give you some excellent referrals for reps or rep organizations they have used.

Regional gift shows are also a great place to solicit sales reps. Booths at these types of shows are often run by sales reps or rep groups that may be willing to talk with you about representing your line of products.

Gift marts or showrooms, unlike gift shows, house numerous rooms where gift wares are showcased all year round. Many of these rooms are run by larger sales rep companies that may be looking for new products. NOTE: Gift shows and gift marts are not open to the public. Check any show or showroom before you visit to find out their specific requirements for visitation.

Trade magazines: In the back of these magazines, you may find a 'Want Ads' listing where you may find a sales rep company specifically looking for new lines.

Sales rep referral or matching organizations are one of these best options for finding a sales representative for your products. These organizations host a listing of sales representation looking for new produce lines. Most of these organizations have websites with lots of helpful information to help you with your search.

Below is a list of some of the most popular referral organizations:

UAMR: http://www.uamr.com

RepHunter: http://www.rephunter.net

GreatRep: http://www.greatrep.com

Manufacturer's Representatives Wanted: http://www.manufacturersrepresentatives.com

Manufacturer's Representative Profile: http://www.mrpusa.com/

Sales Agent USA: http://www.salesagentusa.com/

www.findfashionrep.com

Trade shows and showrooms—you can either 'walk the show' or visit their website for a listing of showrooms and sales reps. Once you find a showroom in your category, you can contact them and see if they are taking on new lines. A few places to start with are the *New York International Gift Fair, the Dallas Market Center, California Market Center* or *Chicago Merchandise Mart.*

Before working with a sales rep, there are a few things you need to keep in mind:

Sales reps work on commission—for an apparel business it's usually 15% of any sales that they make; for bath and beauty products or accessories, for example, it can be 20%. But the average commission is 10-20%.

Sales reps need free samples, marketing materials and anything else to help them sell your products—before working with a sales rep, you need to make sure that you have budgeted for free samples and have created marketing materials to send them to support them during their sales efforts. So you'll need to make a bit of an investment before deciding to work with a sales rep.

You need to constantly communicate with and check in with your sales reps—the more you keep in touch with and communicate with your sales rep(s), the better they perform and the more sales they bring in. You might want to schedule it in your calendar to follow up with them every week or every two weeks or once a month, depending on your needs and schedule.

Also, before you decide to hire a sales rep, make sure you contact some of the other vendors they represent and see how they like working with them, what kind of sales volume they are bringing in and if they recommend that particular sales rep.

Using A Fulfilment House

Do you have plenty of product but not enough space to store it? Is the time you spend filling and shipping orders interfering with the time you'd like to spend on other aspects of your business? Or you'd love help with shipping your orders, but you really don't want to employ anyone else as you're perfectly happy to continue to work on your own from home? If so, it may be time to consider using a fulfillment house!

Having a fulfillment house take care of the storage and shipping of your products allows you to avoid dealing with all of the issues associated with shipping lots of product yourself, and frees you up to take care of the other key aspects of your business—making and selling your products!

While working with a fulfillment house has its own financial implications, if it can allow you to continue to work from home and avoid the need for employees, or a studio or office premises, so could be money well spent.

What does a fulfillment house do? The answer to this question is simple: a fulfillment house stores your stock and ships all your orders for you.

How Does It All Work?

Getting set up with a fulfillment house can be fairly time consuming and involve a financial investment, but once you are up and running the freedom it can give you to concentrate on other parts of your business can be well worth the investment.

Each product that you produce will need to be allocated a product number, and labelled accordingly. Once you make it, you then ship all of your product to the fulfillment house for them to enter into their systems, and they then rack it all on an area of shelving allocated to your business.

When you receive orders via your own online store or shopping cart, you forward these to your fulfillment house at pre-agreed intervals. Depending on your volume of orders, this could be daily, or every few days. The fulfillment house will usually issue you with a password to allow you to access their system online, and you will upload your order information to their server for processing. All of their systems are designed so that as much as possible of the process is automated, so you will have to be willing to listen and learn and upload the information to them in the correct format. This isn't as complicated as it sounds, and during your set-up process a member of their team will guide you through all of this.

Each month, they will bill you and also provide things like stock reports, sales breakdowns etc. so you can keep an eye on stock levels, best-selling items and so on.

How Much Does A Fulfillment House Cost?

Different fulfillment houses have different fee structures, and they will often tailor their fee structures to individual clients. When you consider using a fulfillment house, you should be absolutely clear about how fees will be structured and when payments will be made.

Types of fees that fulfillment houses might charge:

Set-up fees: The bulk of the work of using a fulfillment house happens at the start, when they have to set you and all your products up on their internal systems, and unload and rack all of your stock items. Because of the time involved in this, most companies will impose a fee to cover costs of setting you up. This could run into a few thousand dollars, so you need to get a quote from them right at the start and be sure you can afford this at this stage of your business.

Order processing/packing fees: One of the most common fees charged by fulfillment houses, order processing fees reflect the cost of picking items off the shelves and preparing and packaging them ready for shipping. Often there may be a set charge for packing one item, with a reduction for subsequent items in each package i.e. they may charge $1.00 to pick and pack the first item, and 50c for each subsequent item. A set cost for packaging materials will also be added to each order handled.

Shipping fees: A good fulfillment house will be able to provide you with their shipping rates (which, due to their bulk ordering can often be cheaper than you may pay), and the cost of shipping each item will also be recharged to you. They will be able to ship and track international orders too.

Minimums: Some fulfillment houses enforce their minimum order standards through fees charged if the minimum is not met. At the start it's hard to know just how many orders you will generate, so if you are concerned about having to pay a minimum fee, consider using a fulfillment house with a different minimum or negotiate to have no minimum fees for the first 6-12 months.

Return processing fees: As they will spend time unpacking any returned items and logging them back onto the system, a fulfillment house might have a fee similar to the order processing fee for any returned items.

Storage fees: This is the fulfillment house's charge for holding your products. This is usually charged per shelf or 'bay' and calculated monthly. To keep storage charges from getting too high, you should have the fulfillment house keep only two or three months' inventory of your product on hand.

Hourly rate for extra services: This will cover any work not included in other fees.

In discussing a fulfillment house's fee structure, you should also find out how long the contract will be and what options you have for escaping the contract if the relationship is not working.

PROs And CONs Of Using A Fulfilment House

Pros

Frees you up to concentrate on your business

Gets your stock out of your home or studio

Allows you to deal with busy periods and large orders

No limits on storage space or stock levels

No need to hire employees to help with shipping

Can grow with you as your business grows

Cons

Set-up costs

Requires you to label all products and ship to fulfillment house

Storage and packing costs—compare to doing it yourself or employing someone

Adding that personal touch like a hand-written note, will no longer be possible

Including free stickers or business cards will cost you— they'll be classed as an 'additional item'

Cost to return items and close account if you decide to pull out

Work/Life Balance

Now that your business is growing, it's quite likely that you'll readily admit that it seems to have taken over your life. When you're passionate about what you do, you'll happily spend every waking moment working towards your dreams. But it's impossible to keep the adrenaline and crazy working hours of those first few years going in the long term. Not only will you burn out, but your personal life will suffer, and no amount of business success is worth losing your health, friends or family for. It's time to review how you work, and look at any changes that could be made now to help you move forward in a healthier and happier way.

Busy Vs Productive

Possibly the biggest challenge when you're self-employed is knowing the difference between busy and productive. It's very easy to be busy, there really is never nothing to do when you work for yourself. But being productive means having something to work on that will bring some money in or, at least, directly lead to earning some money.

Know the difference between being busy and being productive.

One will keep you tired. The other will make you money.

You can spend 8 hours straightening/cleaning/re-arranging your desk or studio space. Were you busy? Yep. Tired? Probably.

But it wasn't really "productive." It didn't help you make money. But, at the end of the day, you'll feel like you've "worked."

On the other hand, you could spend those same 8 hours making or photographing some new designs, or emailing 20 buyers at stores you'd love to get your products into.

THAT can help you make money and grow your business.

Now I'm not suggesting that you have to be on full-on capitalist business building mode 24/7—we all need days just to dream, create and kick back—but it's important to step back and look at how you structure your business days and see if there is a way you can make improvements.

What are the things that keep you busy, but are not necessarily productive?

Could your working day be structured better so that you work *SMARTER* not *HARDER*?

The reality is, there's usually only a small fraction of the day when we work to our full potential. Then we tend to drift, lose focus and waste time on other distractions.

Personally, although I can take some time to get going, I know that I am at my most productive and focused in the mornings and my attention span drifts in the afternoons. So I have structured my days to allow half an hour to check in on emails and things like facebook when I first sit at my desk while I ease into the day, and get a few cups of strong tea down me! Then from 9am–1.30pm I focus entirely on writing, then break for lunch. I then go for a 30 min walk around my local park to blow away the cobwebs, then spend my afternoons updating my blog, connecting with others, and enjoying the social networking aspect of promoting my blog and books. This works for me, but it's taken me years to get to the point where I recognized my strengths and weaknesses and found a way to work that gets the best out of me each day.

Have a think about when you work best, what tasks you have each day, and how you may be able to structure your working day to maximize your time.

Don't forget to factor in time for lunch and a stroll. I've also included a section for Personal tasks as you may have children to factor into your day, or other commitments outside the business that you need to work around.

Once you've completed this, pin it somewhere you will see every day and feel free to adapt and tweak your schedule until you find one that works for you!

Your Working Day

	Personal Tasks	Work tasks
8am		
9		
10		
11		
12		
1pm		
2		
3		
4		
5		
6		
Evenings		

Things To Do and Things To Don't!!!

Ever since my first junior admin job, I've used a *To Do* list to guide my working day. If it's not written down in front of me, it's too easy for me to forget. I stock up on beautiful spiral-bound notebooks that I call my "day book," and create a list each day of tasks that need to be done. At the end of each day, I write up the list for the following day, and include any tasks that need to be rolled over from that day. I'm so tragic that I even hang onto all my old day books! Every so often I will flick through an old one, and looking back to tasks from a year or two ago can be an amazing way to remind yourself how far you and your business have come!

To Do List Tips!

- Prioritize your project/task list. I usually list the most important or daunting things each day first, then work down to those that may be less urgent and could potentially be done the next day if time runs out.

- Don't do the easiest thing first. In most cases, when you start with the easier, non-pressing tasks, you are just getting something out of the way that can probably wait.

- Only check your emails 2 or 3 times a day. By only opening your inbox at set intervals and dealing with emails there and then, you'll stay focused on other tasks and avoid the constant distractions of emails pinging in your inbox every few minutes!

- Close your door. Don't be shy about closing your door for an hour here and there during your day if you need to.

- Don't procrastinate. If there is a project or task that you need to tackle, don't put off starting on it, even if it isn't the most pleasant or fun thing on your agenda. And, if it is one of the projects that you haven't begun simply because it's so large or daunting that you don't know where or how to begin, sometimes the best thing to do is to break it down into smaller tasks and deal with it in bite-sized chunks!

- Ask for help. If you are too overloaded, you might not accomplish anything at all. It's okay to ask for help.

- Does it have to be done right now? Does it even have to be done today...or this week? This is an important question to ask anytime anything new hits your desk. Sometimes it will simply be up to you to evaluate its importance, so if it can wait, by all means, let it wait.

- Set aside time for *Facebook*—and avoid it during other times. It's too easy to get sucked in!

Don't Get Burnt Out

When I first started my business, I was so passionate about it, and so keen to grab every opportunity that I could, that I was happy to work as many hours in the day as was physically possible. Evenings, weekends, days, weeks and months all rolled by, and before I knew it several years had passed. All I did was eat, sleep, breathe and talk about my business. Fortunately, my friends and family were amazing and very supportive, but I think, looking back, for them the novelty quickly wore off and, especially as they didn't really "get" or understand my creative business, they soon stopped asking or really listening to me as I banged on about my latest trade show or exciting new product range. No wonder really, I had become a business bore!

While the business was growing and so many exciting and rewarding things were happening for me, I didn't see this as a problem. I was running on adrenaline and sheer ambition, blissfully unaware of the brick wall of burn-out that I was heading straight towards, at high speed!

Just Say No!

If you're burned out, you're no good to your clients, to yourself or those you love. Taking on more work than you can handle, twisting yourself into knots to meet unreasonable deadlines, running scared all of the time…none of this will help you build a long-lasting, rewarding and enjoyable career as your own boss.

If your plate is already full, know when to turn down new work. Also know when to say, "Wow, that is a really great order, and I'd love to supply you with these products, but I couldn't deliver them for 4 more weeks. Would that fit your schedule?" Any decent retailer will happily wait for the right products.

Of course, if something really is an emergency, feel free to take it on. But don't make a habit of this because burnout will be right around the corner. Learn how to pace yourself. Definitely declare at least one day a week as totally work-free, and, yes, that means no checking e-mail. Take a vacation. Spend an entire weekend with your friends or family.

Onwards And Upwards!

Hopefully, if you've made it to the end of this book, you've found at least something useful or inspiring to take away with you. I've tried to cover the very basics for those just getting started, and also some ideas about how to move things forward and cope as your business grows. There are of course so many other aspects of running and growing a business that there just isn't the room to cover in one book, but I hope that this will at least inspire you to take the plunge and move forward with your own crafty business dreams!

I'd love you to join me at www.craftbusinesscommunity.com to share more tips, resources and ideas, and network with other crafty entrepreneurs like yourself—let's grow together and work together to make our creative dreams come true!

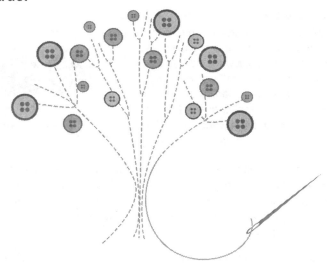

Read on to discover how some other lovely Crafty Entrepreneurs built their businesses—and took their own crafty ideas from dream to reality!

oliver + s

Name: **Liesl Gibson**

Company Name: **Liesl + Co. (Oliver + S and Lisette sewing patterns)**

Founded in: **2007**

Location: **Brooklyn, NYC**

No. of Employees: **4 staff and several freelancers**

Website: **www.oliverands.com/www.sewlisette.com**

After earning a degree in fashion design from the Fashion Institute of Technology (FIT) in NYC, Liesl Gibson worked as a designer for several top fashion brands, including Tommy Hilfiger and Ralph Lauren.

In 2008 Liesl + Co. launched its first brand, Oliver + S, which produces patterns, fabrics, and other products for sewing children's clothing. Oliver + S products are available on the company's website and through independent fabric stores worldwide. Liesl + Co. launched the Lisette brand of patterns and fabric in the spring of 2011, and Liesl's first book, *Oliver + S Little Things to Sew*, which features 20 full-length projects for children's accessories, was published by STC Craft-Melanie Falick Books in 2011.

In 2010 she was given the FabShop Network's Rising Star Award, an honor bestowed by independent fabric store owners across North America.

Tell us how the idea for Oliver + S came about?

You know, I never intended to start a company that produced sewing patterns. But here's where I am today.

Before my daughter was born, I was a fashion designer in New York. After I had her, it just wasn't feasible for me to go back to work full-time. My husband was traveling four days a week for his job, and I did really want to spend more time with my daughter.

So, to keep entertained, I gave myself the challenge of designing and sewing a new wardrobe for my daughter each season. I began by looking at the children's sewing patterns that were available in the market, and nothing inspired me to sew. So, since I had the pattern making skills, I started to make my own designs for her. I had just started a blog, and I began posting photos of what I made for her. People began asking me if they could buy the patterns, and I would occasionally get stopped by someone on the street who asked where I got my daughter's clothes.

A friend encouraged me to make my patterns available for sale. My husband helped me write a business plan. And after a long time spent doing market research and product development, I launched Oliver + S with four pattern styles for little girls.

Did you continue to work while you launched the business?

I think it took well over a year from when I first started writing the business plan until we had product available. I was my daughter's primary caregiver during this time, and I was working on the company with all the free time I had. I put in a lot of very late nights during that year and was exhausted much of the time.

In the early days, I worked on the business myself, but I had input and assistance from several people. My husband was a management consultant at the time, and he helped with the business plan. Brooke Reynolds created our brand identity, packaging, website design, and first trade show booth. She was instrumental in creating the distinctive style that Oliver + S has.

Once we launched and had product to sell, I hired a part-time assistant to help with filling orders and other office-related tasks. It wasn't until we had grown quite a bit that my husband left his job and joined me in the business as the first full-time employee beside me.

Describe the space you work from now? How does this compare to when your first started?

We have studio and office space now in an old, converted industrial building in Brooklyn. Our whole floor of the building used to be a book bindery, and we have old sewing needles embedded into the cracks in the floor between the wood floor boards. I've always thought this is a nice touch for our sewing space!

When I started Oliver + S, I was working from our small apartment in Manhattan. But we quickly determined that I needed a dedicated workspace. When I was working, I would cover all available surfaces in our small apartment with my pattern making paper and tools, and there was no room for anyone else. So taking a commercial space became an imperative pretty quickly for us. If we lived in the suburbs and had a large house with an extra bedroom or two, I wouldn't have had to take a commercial work space as quickly as I did.

Your business has now grown considerably and you have some great staff on board. At what point did you know you needed help?

There are two main reasons to add staff to a small growing business, and we've added staff for both of them. Either you have so much work you need to do that you can't do it all and you find you need assistance. Or you find the right person and you decide that bringing that person on board will allow you to take on new challenges and grow the business beyond where it is at present.

Your online store is beautiful and has various functions beyond just selling patterns. How important is it to invest in a good website?

I've been fortunate to have a business partner who is good at technology, which is very important for our business. He was instrumental in getting our website set up and growing it slowly over time to have more functionality. We've found that it's very important to have a website that is about more than just selling product. Our website is our most cost effective way of marketing our business, so we've invested in features there that will get people to engage with the brand and keep returning.

You now supply your patterns to hundreds of stores internationally. How did you achieve this? Do you show at any trade shows?

The growth trajectory for the Oliver + S brand has been slow and steady. Most of our wholesale customers are long-term customers, and we grow by having new stores pick up the line. We sell the Oliver + S products solely into the independent fabric store market, and that industry has one major trade show that occurs twice a year, International Quilt Market. We exhibit at this show. That was where we got our first exposure to the wholesale customer base, and we continue to show there to keep the market aware of our newest products. Most distributors from countries outside the US attend this show, and that's how we've established relationships with our distributors around the world.

Trade shows are a lot of work and are quite expensive to do. I'm always exhausted and physically sore when a show is done. There's nothing glamorous about exhibiting at a trade show, believe me. We get approached about exhibiting at other trade shows quite often, but we've never been convinced that the benefits of doing them will offset the costs.

You're an author too (*Oliver + S Little Things to Sew: 20 Classic Accessories and Toys for Children*). Many people dream of securing a book deal – how did you get yours?

For us, the reason we did the book was to expand the range of Oliver + S products in the market and to introduce new customers to the brand. If you are going to take the enormous amount of time it takes to do a book, you need to be sure that you have a reason for doing it. Unless you somehow manage to write the best-selling book of the year in the craft category, you'll end up making less than minimum wage on an hourly basis considering the amount of time you put into writing and marketing the book. Craft books just aren't money making ventures!

I had some insight into how to sell a book proposal because I began my career as a book editor, believe it or not. (After that I spent a few years doing equity research on Wall Street before I returned to school to earn a degree in fashion design.) And I was also fortunate to have some friends who had published craft books and were willing to coach me on what was expected in a craft book proposal.

When I was ready to shop the book around, I put together a pitch book for the concept which included information about the Oliver + S brand, a proposed table of contents, some sample project materials, and a biography of me. I made a list of the publishing houses that I could see taking the book and got in touch with the craft editors there. There were several publishers that bid on the book, and we then had a hard decision to make about which offer to accept. For us, because this was intended to be a brand-building project, being able to publish a book that "felt" like Oliver + S was even more important to us than the royalty rate and the advance offered. We eventually went with the publisher that we thought would be the best fit. And we've been very happy with how the book turned out.

You're now also and award-winning fabric designer and on your 3rd collection for Moda. Congratulations! How did this come about?

Well, I've won an industry award, and I've designed fabric collections, but I wouldn't consider myself an award-winning fabric designer!

Finding a manufacturer to license a fabric collection is much the same as finding a publisher to publish a book. When I decided it was time to produce an Oliver + S line of fabric, I put together concepts for the first collection I wanted to do. I then made a list of the manufacturers who I thought would be interested in the line, and I arranged meetings with their design directors.

Again, deciding on whom to work with came down to more than just the money. We ultimately made the decision to work with Moda for the fabric line because of how that relationship would help the Oliver + S brand overall.

In 2011, while Oliver + S was still growing, you launched a completely new brand called Lisette. Why did you decide to do that?

I had always wanted to do a women's apparel sewing line, but I faced a problem. There are two different distribution channels for sewing products—independent stores and chain stores. We designed Oliver + S to be sold only through independent stores. The problem is that the majority of apparel sewing in the US is done with products purchased at chain stores. Independent stores, for the most part, are quilting stores that carry printed cotton. (All the Oliver + S patterns are designed to be sewn with printed cottons, so they can be sold by quilt stores that carry only that kind of fabric.) But I wanted to do a line of sewing patterns and fabrics that would include apparel fabrics like lawn, canvas, twill, corduroy, etc. Most independent stores don't carry these kinds of fabrics, so the line I envisioned wasn't possible to produce for the same market as Oliver + S sells in.

I knew we needed to work with the chain stores to bring this line to market, since they are the only stores that carry these apparel fabrics. But I also knew that the chain stores are not interested in working with small companies like ours. From their perspective there's too much risk working with small companies, and they don't want to have business relationships with thousands of little companies. So I knew we needed to find partners for this brand.

We pitched the idea for this new brand to a contact we had at Fabric Traditions, which is a major fabric supplier to chain stores. She liked the idea and was interested in producing the fabric. She provided an introduction to the team at Simplicity which has a strong presence on the sewing pattern side with the chains, and we presented the idea to them. They were interested as well. So we approached Jo-Ann stores here in the United States first because they are the largest chain. They were excited by the concept, so we developed the line primarily for them—at first. Now you can also purchase Lisette products at other places as well. The Lisette fabrics are now available at the Spotlight chain in Australia, and Lisette patterns are available anywhere worldwide that Simplicity patterns are sold.

We couldn't have developed and launched this brand without our business partners, and they provide a lot of support in producing the pattern and fabric line.

You've been lucky enough to gain tons of press coverage. Did/do you do your own PR?

When I first launched the company, I hired a PR consultant who works in the fabric industry to help get word out about the company. Results on that effort were mixed. It cost a lot, and at the end of the day the coverage that resulted probably wasn't worth the investment.

Since then, we've done all our own PR in-house. We'll provide samples of new product each season to select fabric manufacturers, magazine and website publishers, and bloggers. But it's not magazine coverage that sells patterns these days. It's people writing about their experience sewing with a pattern on their blogs. We can tell the moment a prominent blogger posts something about one of our patterns because we start getting an unusual volume of website orders flowing in for one item.

To get people to want to blog about your product, you have to have a great product that people love and enjoy using. These testimonials are the best form of endorsement a product can get, and they really do encourage other people to buy the item too.

You blog, and both Oliver + S and Lisette have great online presences. Flickr groups, Facebook, Twitter – How do you find the time?!

There's never enough hours in the day. We would really like to do much more with the blogs on both the Oliver + S and Lisette sites, but if we did it would take time away from developing new product which is, after all, what pays the bills. But keeping your brand in front of your customers with good blog content, interesting Tweets, useful Facebook wall posts, etc. is just good business. So we make the time to do this, but we wish we could do even more.

I really do enjoy this aspect of running a business. One of my greatest pleasures is looking through the photos that get posted in our Oliver + S Flickr group and seeing so many happy children wearing our styles. I love it that I can help people create unique, one-of-a-kind items for their children and grandchildren and I love to see the results of what our customers do with my patterns.

Liesl Gibson's
Top Ten Tips
for Creative Business Success

1) Develop a solid business plan before starting your business.

2) Manage your business to that plan.

3) Produce the best, highest quality product that you can.

4) Find the time to feed your creative spirit while running your company.

5) Provide excellent customer service.

6) Be reliable; deliver what you promise when you promised to deliver it.

7) Hire experts (a lawyer, accountant, web developer, customer service professional, etc.) to help you out in areas where you don't have expertise or interest.

8) Never believe your own press; you're only as good as the next product you create.

9) Market yourself and your business effectively; don't be a wallflower, but don't be bold and brash either.

10) Always look for partnership opportunities that will provide you and your prospective partner with a win-win.

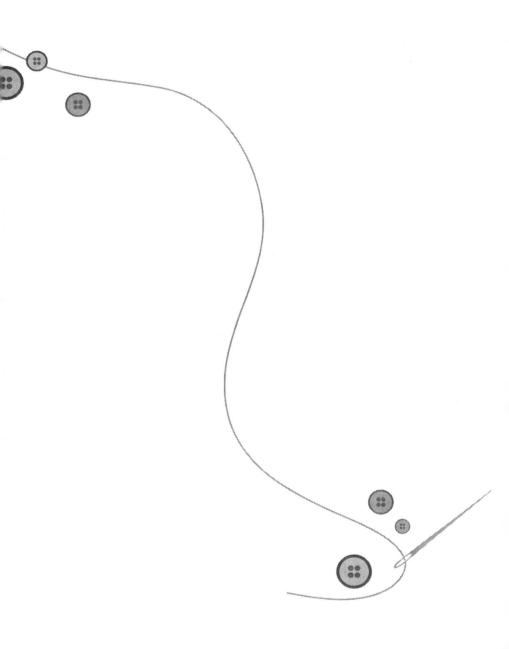

Name: **Gillian Harris**

Company Name: **Gilliangladrag**

Founded in: **2000**

Location: **Surrey, UK**

No. of Employees: **8**

Website: **www.gilliangladrag.co.uk**

I used to be a very busy graphic designer working in the TV and video industry until I had my second daughter in 1998 and jubilantly announced that "enough was enough". With my family's roots in tailoring and the rag trade, I was very pleased to then have the opportunity to pursue my love of textiles and shortly afterwards I fell head over heels into feltmaking!

My triumphant first felt book 'Complete Feltmaking' was published in 2006, and I have just written my second book 'Carnival of Felting'. I live in Capel, Surrey with my un-felted husband Chris, my two daughters Polly & Rosie, and our dog BettyBoo. In 2010 I moved our flourishing business to a new headquarters "The Fluff-a-torium" in nearby Dorking. Which quite frankly has been fantastic, and the family are now finding a lot less fluff in their dinner!

Having persuaded some big retailers to sell our fantastic products, myself and some other very important Fluff-a-tiers are now happily operating our business from Dorking and selling all manner of wondrous fluffy things, in between teaching and doing our very best to be rather inspirational!

From graphic design to felt-making—that's quite a career change! How did it all come about?

I think I'd secretly always had a bit of an obsession with textiles, and it sat neatly alongside my other design work. I have very early memories of making my best friend a felt mouse, about age 5. One grandfather was a tailor and the other was in the rag trade, so it was only a matter of time before my fluffy gene emerged! Once I could legitimately resign from graphic design (due to the birth of my second daughter) I found it difficult to sit still for too long. It would appear I can't just "get on" with something as a hobby. I get slightly obsessive about what I do and some might say I'm a workaholic, so it wasn't long before my career path had taken a different direction!

Describe the space you work from...how do you make it inspiring as well as functional?

My workspace does say a lot about me. It has to be adorned with all my favorite things and pieces of work, plus the work of others that I admire. I couldn't even contemplate operating from a temporary space that I couldn't make my own— it would be soul destroying. My space has to reflect everything about me and is a continuation of my work. My workspace is extremely colorful—very fluffy, slightly chaotic—and I'm extremely "creatively" messy, but I do like a slightly organized mess. Everything is to hand. (Well, at least I know where it is!)

You now have your very own shop, 'The Fluff-a-torium'! A store is a big
financial outlay – you must have been very confident it would work!

Well, it was a case of finding somewhere "proper" to operate from, before my
long suffering husband lost the plot. The business had taken over literally every
corner of not only my studio, but our whole house! The day that he couldn't get
through the front door due to 100 cardboard boxes that had been delivered was
a bit of a turning point, and we knew we had to look for premises.

The shop and studio that we now operate from are obviously a huge overhead
and have added a lot to my workload too, but I waited as long as I could before
I took the plunge, and felt confident that I had enough strings to my bow before
signing on the dotted line. I see our shop as our premises, and our headquarters,
and our showroom, and our teaching space—so it isn't "just" a shop—it serves
our business on a lot of different levels.

I sometimes feel like I fly by the seat of my pants a little, but I had also done my
homework and knew that I had a solid business behind me. Having grown my
business quite organically over many years it didn't feel as overwhelmingly mad
as it would have been if I was new to it all!

Advice and tips for those considering a new shop or premises—it's absolutely
VITAL to work out how much money you will need to take every day, just to
break even. That will bring you back down to earth! That means doing a serious
business plan and really thinking things through. It's too easy to get carried away
without thinking through the realities.

You are a mum to two teenage daughters. How do you manage to balance
running a business with being a mum?

My two girls are now age 14 and 17, and I have to say that I couldn't do what
I do now when my two girls were younger. Working from my studio at home to
start with, allowed me to "juggle" family life with working. Now they are older
I am able to be away from home for longer. They are both very supportive and
understanding, and I think they appreciate how hard I work. Polly now works in
the shop for me on a Saturday and Rosie has started to do a little work for me
too, so they like to be involved and I appreciate their input.

When I was operating from home I was able to separate what I did from the
family because I was lucky enough to have a beautiful studio in our garden at
the back of the house. We rigged up a baby alarm so I could hear what was
going on and could "talk to the house" (you know, to stop arguments and send
people to bed etc!) but at the same time I could run in and start cooking in
between working.

I'm quite good at multi- tasking and many people I know are amazed at how much I do and the amount of stuff I can cram into one day. Inevitably, some things have suffered as a result of me running a business and being so busy all the time, but on the whole I made every parents evening and school play! I like to be in control, so working for myself has always been ideal.

Do you produce all of your felting kits yourself? How did you source all the components and find the right wholesalers?

Yes, we do produce all our kits ourselves. Having worked with wool and felt for so long I knew where to source everything. I am no longer personally involved with actually physically putting the kits together and have some lovely Fluff-a-tiers who do this now. Being the control freak that I am however, I would find it extremely difficult to outsource this, so when we have a large order, we quite simply employ more staff and increase productivity. The potential of outsourcing still exists, but for now our operation works for us.

You run tons of great felting workshops at your Fluff-a-torium. How have these been going? Any tips for designers considering offering workshops while they build the other aspects of their business. Is it worth all the effort?

I do run a lot of courses at the Fluff, and this has always been a core part of my business and something I enjoy immensely. I think a lot of workshop customers come to me because they have seen or read my first book 'Complete Feltmaking' and because they admire what I do. My customers often come on more than one workshop, partly because they want to further different feltmaking skills, and partly because they have a jolly good time—or so I am told!

How have you financed the growth of your company – did you have to approach the banks for loans?

I am quite hard-nosed when it comes to money, and don't take financial matters lightly when it's my neck on the line at the end of the day. I have been in the extremely fortunate position of never having to borrow a penny, but that is because I have ploughed every penny back into the company and grown it from nothing over many years. I know that I have a real driving force and love of what I do that keeps me going. You need to have a vision, and make sure that you keep focused on your goals.

I also feel very strongly that you shouldn't sell yourself and what you do too cheaply. Whilst it's incredibly flattering to sell an item of work or get new customers, you will soon learn that it's COMPLETELY POINTLESS selling things too cheaply.

I always despair at those who sell handmade items for virtually no money. If it's just a hobby and you enjoy it, then that's fine, but if you are running a business, that is business suicide. Early on, decide how much your time is worth and make sure you factor that in alongside everything else when costing your products—especially if you are making them yourself.

Whilst I appreciate that it's worth offering a discount to a potentially large customer I always remember my wise husband's chant: *"Turnover is Vanity, Profit is Sanity"*. That is very true. It's pointless getting a massive order and bragging about it if you make no money!

Your kits and packing have such a unique and individual look. Have your designs or ideas ever been copied/ripped off?

All of my products are protected by "ACID", and whilst to my knowledge—as I write —no one has come close to copying my packaging or my branding, unfortunately one particular product design of mine was imitated in a different colorway and turned into a kit. A lot of the other elements from my business were also copied, which was shocking and upsetting.

Several third parties contacted me to draw my attention to what was going on. They felt that the similarity of this work to my own may have caused confusion within the niche marketplace that we operated in. Sadly, we found ourselves unable to take legal action on this occasion, which was very frustrating. They say that imitation is the sincerest form of flattery, but it can also be a very bitter pill to swallow when you feel like someone has literally "taken a piece of you". Somewhat ironically, as part of the same case, it was also brought to my attention that a number of others were also imitating my designs in their businesses too!

Intellectual Property Rights law is very complicated, but at least it can protect designers if their work has been copied in detail. When you spend your time and creative energy coming up with new ideas and creating new designs—in order to inspire and educate—it is immensely upsetting when someone uses what you've done in a way that you hadn't intended. I never imagined that someone would actually mimic my creative style and my designs, and I would definitely recommend protecting your ideas and designs as much as you can.

Whilst anything like this makes me literally BOIL with rage, it's worth bearing in mind that anyone who needs to copy your work so closely must surely possess little creativity themselves. I think that my time and energy is better focused positively on my creativity, rather than on what others are doing!

I think what also helped me, was the realization that however wrong, every successful brand and designer tends to get copied and imitated to some extent, and yet they still become, and remain successful. They are the leaders, not the followers. They are the creators of the unique desirable designs. I feel confident and positive about my own creativity, and you should too if you're going into business, as that's what it's all about.

The best piece of advice I was given was from my mother's cousin's 85 year old boyfriend from New York about 13 years ago! I can't exactly remember his precise words, but he looked at one of the bags I had made (and was selling) all those years ago, and commented on the fact that:

a) He liked it (which was a pretty good start) and

b) I was never going to make much money if I was going to make them all myself.

Initially I dismissed what he said, but it made me think. I'm not entirely sure how it has shaped what I do now, and I'm not for one minute suggesting that you should get someone else to do all your hard work, but it was interesting advice at the time.

I guess that what he said underlies a way of thinking, making sure that what you do makes sound business sense. If it's a business that you want to have, own, run (rather than just a hobby) then you need to think and behave in a business-like way. Because at the end of the day—the buck stops with YOU!

And finally...what does the future hold for Gilliangladrag...any exciting plans you'd like to share?

I do have big plans for Gilliangladrag! All the ideas in my head rarely leave me alone, as I can't just be content with what I've achieved so far! I'm not going to go into much detail as it would be highly embarrassing if my plans didn't come to fruition! What I will say is that I hope that my brand will continue to grow and become respected and sought after—all around the world.

Hand Embroidered
Heirlooms of the Future

Name: **Jan Constantine**

Company Name: **Jan Constantine Ltd**

Founded in: **2002**

Location: **Cheshire, UK**

No. of Employees: **10 Full Time, 5 Part Time**

Website: **www.janconstantine.com**

Jan Constantine is a UK-based home-ware designer whose patriotic designs and bold motifs have become her signature and are stocked in hundreds of boutiques around the world.

Jan spent her early career as a successful fashion designer in London, UK. After 10 years she relocated to the Cheshire countryside and was inspired to move into interior design. Her homes have been featured in many prestigious home magazines and she has appeared on several TV shows, and she has also worked as a stylist on magazines such as Italian Vogue and W Magazine and various ad campaigns.

What began as a small business sewing lavender hearts around her kitchen table with friends quickly grew.

Her hand embroidery business has now grown into an established brand—today, Jan's designs are stocked in Liberty of London, Selfridges, Fortnum & Mason, Harrods and boutiques in Britain and the USA, with new product lines planned. In 2011 Jan's second book 'Love Stitching' was published in the UK by Jacqui Small and in the USA by Stash Books.

Tell us a bit about your design/career background, and how your company came about?

I used to make cushions for Christmas and birthday presents—everyone loved them and said I should go into business and sell them. I originally started my business around the kitchen table stitching lavender bags with friends, with the odd bottle of wine. I was known for my embellished and embroidered designs when I was in the fashion industry and I carried this over to the designs for my cushions and lavender hearts.

Your cushions and textiles are hand embroidered and you're a strong supporter of preserving these traditional skills. Tell us about how your products are made, and how did you find your very talented workforce?

I soon realized that if I was to be successful then I would have to have my designs made abroad. Although some of my products are made in the UK there is only a very limited number of hand-embroiderers here, so I had to make several trips to India to find the right people to work for me. My products are made using traditional skills that are passed from father to son over the generations. We work mainly with a company that interprets what I need using natural fabrics and old fashioned stitching techniques. I went through at least half a dozen factories until I found the one I needed to interpret ideas and high quality.

Your HQ is based in the Cheshire countryside. Sounds idyllic! Describe to us your workplace now, and how this differs to when you first started out?

When I first started it was on the kitchen table at home, sewing with a few friends. Then we moved into an old renovated stable block. Now we work from two offices, one in the stable block which is near to my house and one at a warehouse about 5 miles away, where we now pack and dispatch.

You also design ceramics, stationery, nightwear etc. Who manufactures these for you?

We had a disaster with the first ceramics company not being able to fulfill orders and demand. We now have a licensing program that we are developing with specialist companies that produce stationery, textiles, candles, bed linen and gift wrap etc. I found it was very trial and error to begin with but now I have consultants to help me.

With such a wide range of products, that's a lot of stock! How do you store and distribute it all? Do you use a fulfillment warehouse? Do you still ship all your own orders?

We ship all our own orders for our core product from our warehouse. Our licensed products are dispatched from the licensee's warehouse to the trade accounts (we just deal with our web orders and exhibition stock).

Stock can be a nightmare if you don't control it properly. Regular stock counts and clear outs should be routine. I try to 'throw out' old lines when I introduce new ones to keep stock down but I'm constantly being asked for my archive numbers to be revived by stores, so this can be tricky. In future I would like to change to a fulfillment house as there are so many overheads with our own warehouse and the business is changing the way it works.

Your products are stocked all over the world—how did you make the leap from supplying to UK shops into supplying internationally?

My Local Chamber of Commerce and the DTI (Department for Trade and Industry) helped us by offering workshops, expert advice and grants. WIRE (Women in Rural Enterprise) were also helpful to us in the early days of the business. You must endeavor to establish in your own country first and foremost. The New York International Gift Fair was a great platform for us to test the US market, and then sheer determination!

Very expensive, but essential for marketing as well as sales. It is great to be able to launch your new collections and it makes you focus on a deadline. You can display your products how you want the world to see them, keep in touch with buyers and network with other exhibitors and press.

The Spirit of Christmas Fair in London was the first consumer fair I did, and I launched my business there. It wasn't an instant success but I wasn't deterred. My next fair was the UK Trade Show Top Drawer a year later when I was ready to supply trade, and my products were very well received.

A couple of fairs later the Bed and Bath buyer from the famous London store Fortnum and Mason placed an order right on my stand. I was over the moon when she told me who she was—my first London store!

At the next fair I did—The Country Living Fair—the first person on my stand was a buyer from Liberty of London and I nearly fell through the floor! I always loved Liberty, as a student I would spend hours mulling over which print I should spend my allowance on. My English Country Garden designs were on their shelves within weeks! My products still sell in Fortnum & Mason and Liberty today.

The worst exhibition that I ever did was a brand new one at Excel in London's Docklands. It looked great but was an utter disaster. I lost lots of money because there were hardly any people there and they had no money to spend. I wasn't the only person to shed a tear that week—it was so disappointing. I'm very cautious now about new fairs that aren't tried and tested. Even established ones, I always check out by walking the floor and getting feedback from several companies prior to booking anything that I haven't tried before.

In the early days I used to stay up most of the night preparing price lists and press packs. I used to be so nervous on the stand and it took several shows before I had enough confidence to approach buyers to ask if they needed help—I was terrified! I used to find the first day of a show absolutely exhausting—after putting together a new collection, driving down to London, setting up the stand myself and then presenting the collection and myself as poised as possible, I was wiped out! But it has all paid off, and now I have staff to do this for/with me.

Some exhibition organizers are very kind and offer free exhibitor drinks at the end of the first day and often have an award ceremony for best stand in show etc. I always think how great it must be for new exhibitors to win a prize—so encouraging for new start-ups.

I started off as a retail business selling to the consumer so when I started being asked for trade prices I had to do a rethink. Basically I work out exactly what it costs to produce something, have it delivered to me and finished/handled in-house, I then double the price and add on VAT to calculate my trade price. The trade then do the same thing (double it) to get the retail price. This doesn't apply to every customer and every product though—but it's how I started. If I have a very large order I can reduce the price if I can get the components cheaper. Some large UK department store chains do work on a higher mark-up than most, but I'm not always in a position to facilitate that due to the nature of my hand embroidery. It would be different if my products were all made by machine, but my products are more people based.

I began with a family loan of £10,000. Soon when I needed more, I had 2 repeats of that. A short time after, I had two loans from my home mortgage company. I then increased the mortgage on my London crash pad, but then had to rent it out to make the payments. Then I needed to put a lot of money into the business so I pitched to investors who now own 35% of my business after a further investment. A couple of years ago, I had a massive bank loan to help me with the next stage of growth. I've often paid for shows and shipments with my personal credit cards.

To keep on top of the late payments I have a rotweiller called Liz who calls everyone as soon as she sniffs anything overdue and continues to do so! We send a formal letter initially, then a second to warn that we will be taking them to court if they don't pay. We have always been paid except when a famous London store went bust. They started up again in business but we didn't have a chance of recouping our loss. Luckily we put lots of pressure on them prior to them folding and we did get some payment but not all so it pays off to be vigilant. All new accounts I keep on pro forma payment for at least a year or until they spend a certain amount of money with us. Obviously large stores won't pay pro forma, but I don't allow anybody over 30 days. A small company cannot handle 60 days or more.

No—not yet! When I struck the first deal with my publisher she said to me "It won't buy you a house in France" and so far I don't have the money to get that house (in Italy actually). Every spare penny I have goes straight back into the business. It may be successful but it is also very expensive to run.

I received an email from Jacqui Small saying that she'd seen my very lovely work in Liberty and asking if I would be interested in talking about writing a book. I'm thrilled to have just launched my second book. The advances that I have received from my book deals have been treated as my bonus and nothing to do with the business, so I have actually used them for treats for me and my family. You only make lots of money from writing books if they sell very well. You don't see many craft books in the top 100! But you never know! I would always say it's great to have the chance to write a book because it gives you credibility and it makes you the expert in your field.

Your designs are incredibly unique and are instantly recognizable as a "Jan Constantine". How does it feel when obvious copies start springing up on the high street. What have been your experiences of copyright infringement?

I have been copied and passed off by large and small companies and even department stores who you wouldn't dream of—because they like to appear squeaky clean. In my eyes it's stealing, because my designs are so unique, it's so obvious when they're copied.

I'm currently in process of trying to stop a huge high street chain from killing off one of my most successful pieces. I was made aware of it in a press pack from a magazine stylist and we're trying to stop it reaching the shelves. We managed to put a stop to it thanks to the early tip off. I'm a member of ACID (Anti Copying in Design —a UK based organization that works with designers to protect their interests), but quite honestly the cost of using even their discounted lawyer is prohibitive for small companies and designers to go after the big boys.

With the help of one of my consultants I sent a letter pointing out breach of copyright and threatening legal action. The small companies often ignore it and say they've done nothing wrong and it's their own design!! That's when you have to go legal— but if you can make an example of someone, word gets round and others are less likely to copy you. It isn't easy but we have to make a point.

I know it's not probably what I should be saying but if I knew how much money, blood, sweat and tears I would go through before I began my business, I don't think I would have done it!

I have had big problems with people that have worked alongside me too. I'd say be careful with partners or anyone who wants to get into your company—try to remain independent if you can and get the best advice you can afford without compromising your position or business. Power can be a very dangerous thing and when some people see success they want a part of it.

People have advised me all the way and some has been good and some has been bad. In retrospect, if I could do it all again I would have more confidence in myself and not trust certain people so much! As a company grows it's good to learn about shares and investments before they happen—because it can be a can of worms! And if you don't know your stuff and you have an attractive business, you'll be eaten alive by those who want a stake in your business.

The best advice for me is to listen to my gut instinct! If a crisis is happening, it is best for me to get away, to think logically and not to panic—get some good advice from a calm person, not a pessimist. My naivety has cost me a lot of wasted money, effort and time. The best advice has been from people who are impartial and not connected with the business at all.

For the future, the business model is changing. My brand is strong enough now to be licensed into many different products. This is the most exciting thing I have ever done. It is so amazing to see my designs come to market without having to produce them and sell them myself!

My stationery and tin-wear launched recently and it has already sold double what was expected! I love the fact that anyone will be able to buy into the Jan Constantine brand because it's affordable. We've got bags, kitchen textiles, melamine and bed linen in the pipeline and already have china, greeting cards, gift wrap, gift tags and boxes. It's an exciting time!

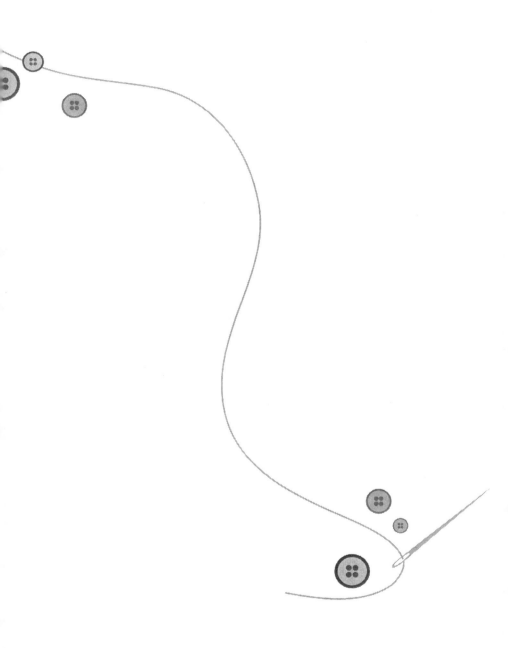

Pick Up Sticks
(jewelry company) *n.*

Name: **Sabrina Colson and Glena Henry**

Company Name: **Pick Up Sticks Jewelry Co. LLC.**

Founded in: **1999**

Location: **Clovis, New Mexico**

No. of Employees: **4**

Website: **www.pickupsticks.net**

Cousins Glena and Sabrina grew up in Logan, a small town in rural New Mexico, population 500. The most entertaining activities in this rural area were swatting flies on their great grandmother's porch, building miniature houses out of rocks and bits of glass, and searching for the perfect smooth stone. Their great grandmother led them to explore a world of tiny hidden treasures, investigate abandoned houses and frontier dumps, while encouraging them to fill their pockets with sticks, stones, glass, feathers, and flowers.

Eventually, Sabrina and Glena each followed their own professional interests: Sabrina concentrated on art and graphic design, while Glena pursued business and education. Ultimately, the two combined their love of family heirlooms, antique finds, and time-worn treasures with their experience in the fields of art and business to start a company of their own, Pick Up Sticks Jewelry Co. LLC. What started as a new business venture has become a way for the cousins to revisit their past and those times spent with their great grandmother in a small town.

You each had your own successful careers before joining forces to launch Pick Up Sticks. Whose idea was it?

Glena had already opened a jewelry store, and I told her that I had an idea for how to combine photos and jewelry, and wanted to know if she would be willing to try to sell some of my pieces. She said yes, so I made about 20 photo charms; they got a lot of attention in her store. At the time, I was living in Arizona and Glena was living in New Mexico, and I heard about a wholesale show. We applied, were accepted, and we quickly realized that we had no idea what we were doing! We didn't know how to write an order, we used waitress ticket books. We had no displays, so we took antiques from my house. We didn't know industry terminology like minimum order, lead time, net 30, or exclusivity, so we had no rules. We wrote a couple of thousand dollars worth of orders, and thought, "we're rich!" But there was the heavy realization that we now had to make all of this jewelry ourselves! Let's just say that Glena and I stayed up until 3am for weeks, there was lots of vodka consumed, and we never got out of our pajamas!

When the business started, were you both still holding down regular jobs?

Yes, Glena was teaching school, and I was working on my student teaching.

Tell us a bit about Pick Up Sticks as it stands today – where are you based?

The studio, lead by Glena is in Clovis, New Mexico. I design remotely (with several visits a year) from Albuquerque, NM. We have 4 women who work flexible hours. I design the pieces myself (original collage using vintage images), with a ton of collaboration from Glena and the ladies in the studio. Our photo charms are framed outside of the country, then we assemble and ship from New Mexico.

Describe the early days of your business?

We were flying by the seat of our pants! The learning curve was like a roller-coaster ride. Traveling to cities where we had never been, going to market, it was fun, exciting and terrifying all at the same time!

How did you make ends meet in those early days, and how long did it take before you were turning a profit?

We were very conservative with supplies, and inventory. Never keeping more than we needed, but always having enough to fill orders. Cheap hotels, working out of our homes, small booths—we could take everything we needed to a trade show in just two suitcases. We were lucky, Pick Up Sticks never "operated in the red" and our only criterion for turning a profit was that we each wanted to at least make a teacher's salary. We accomplished that the first year, but we also only made this amount for several years after that.

At what stage in the business did you take on your first employee?

Right away, during the first year we needed help! We weren't sure we could afford it. But we knew that we wouldn't be able to fulfill our promises to our retailers if we didn't, and we knew that would not be a good business plan.

Manufacturing and sourcing – Do you make every single piece yourself, or employ help now? How has this changed from when you started out?

Again, we really lucked out on this one. A family member was able to put us in touch with the perfect manufacturer at the perfect time. We didn't have to research this one at all. With sourcing components, we had to have a lot of patience at first. Photo charms were being shipped to us with poor printing etc. There were a lot of quality control issues at first. Most of the issues were worked out in the first year. My advice here: just because a manufacturer doesn't get it exactly right the first time (or the second, or the third), don't give up. Have patience, but have a backup plan.

Trade Shows—an expensive, but necessary tool?

Oh yes. But this is how we built our business. No sales reps. We did it all ourselves. Plus, this was before the internet was such a marketing power for small businesses; we couldn't have built our business without wholesale trade show exposure. I'm not going to say, it was so small, but thank goodness that it was. We couldn't have handled a big show with a lot of orders at that time. OK. It was Oasis in Phoenix!

What have been your experiences, from your very first show, right up until now? Any tips for those considering their first big trade show?

Buyers are at market to make important investment decisions, so provide them with helpful information about your line. These are professional, intelligent business people, and they don't need to be pressured. Do not "Sell"—EDUCATE.

When you are tempted to "sell", ask questions instead. What kind of a store do you have? Have you seen our line before? Do you carry anything similar? I know this seems like suicide, but encourage buyers to comparison shop. Ask them to let you know if they find a product that is similar to yours, that is better than yours. This will give you invaluable feedback on your pricing and quality.

Think of your booth backdrop as a billboard. Use beautiful graphics, showing your company name and clear product photographs. Use handouts sparingly, and think small. We give out a postcard with lovely product photography and contact information. We highlight our online catalog. Printing a full catalog is expensive, damn it. Plus, buyers do not want to carry a lot of bulky paperwork.

Have a current customer list; cut the dead wood out before every tradeshow. Serious buyers need to know if there is someone in their area that already carries your line.

Pick your booth location wisely. Research wholesale shows wisely as well, they are expensive, and a bad decision can break the bank. Do a mock booth set-up. Take photographs and take them to the show with you, this will save you a ton of set-up time. And get an "everything box": pens, stapler, tape, scissors, paper, business cards, rubber bands, etc. When you get to a show, it is like a ship-wreck—you will only have the items that you brought with you, so be prepared for everything and anything!

Use the lulls in traffic to network with other exhibitors, and for goodness sake be nice to them. Better yet, make friends with other exhibitors, and refer buyers back and forth. Other exhibitors have become our greatest mentors over the years.

If another exhibitor gets a customer in the booth, make yourself scarce. Exhibitors are at shows to service clients, they didn't come to chitchat with other exhibitors, unless time allows.

We make the joke that if the buyer is not in comfortable shoes, they're not a serious buyer; they are more likely someone who is at market to place personal orders.

You have a great website and sell directly to the public online. You're also stocked by hundreds of independent stores. Discuss the pros and cons of selling directly to the public, vs. wholesaling to retailers?

Wholesale is the bread and butter of our company, and we believe always will be. The bricks and mortar stores that carry our line are the priority. Period. We made the decision a few months ago to start a retail website. We were sensitive about our pricing, and made it higher than our retailers would normally sell for. Yes, the retail margin is higher, but I caution anyone who has a large retail store base, because the retail website orders hardly justify the higher margin for us. The retail website simply does not produce much revenue. The collectors of Pick Up Sticks Jewelry need to touch, feel, play and experiment with different combinations of charms. They just can't do that online; they need to go to a store for that experience. We only provide a retail website to allow collectors a way to find a specific charm that a store may not have in stock.

How many and what sort of stores do you supply to?

We now supply to around 900 in the US, a few hundred in Canada, and are soon to get a distributor in the UK.

How do you ensure you get paid by retailers on time to keep cash-flow moving etc?

From day one, our policy has always been that we will not ship the order until it is paid for. And we do not charge a customer's credit card until the day the jewelry ships. The only exception to this policy is with much larger retail chains, catalogs, and museum stores. Oh yes, and the other exception is with retailers that we have a long history of successful business; we will allow them net 30 terms.

What do you wish you'd know when you started? Is there anything you would do differently?

SHIP!!!!!!!!! Ship orders as fast as you can, fill the order complete. Communicate with your customers, pick up the phone and call them directly, the instant you foresee any problems or changes to the agreed upon plan.

Make it easy for customers to speak to you and encourage them to communicate with you. Give them your direct email address, let your staff give them your phone number if you are not at your desk, and return messages immediately. This is not a person with whom you will be in a short-term relationship; this is not a person you are "selling" to. This is a person who is your partner in business. Respect them, help them, listen to them, and make them happy that they have chosen your company.

I wish I would have known how hard it is to find a good sales representative— we currently don't use any. Same goes for showrooms. We currently have a wonderful distributor in Canada; a good relationship with a distributor can be a big financial benefit.

Highs and Lows. What have been the best and worst things to happen in your business to date?

Best thing? Having a business partner that is freaking awesome! Glena and I compensate for each other's weaknesses, support each other's strengths, and a lot of the time, just stay out of each other's way so that we can do what we are best at. I know that is not something that "happened" to us, but it really is the best thing about Pick Up Sticks.

Worst thing? Doesn't even matter anymore, there is no advice that could have prevented the bad things that have happened, so it is irrelevant. Success is so sweet; I don't want to look back. Look ahead, work fast, learn from your mistakes, and SHIP!

And finally...what does the future hold for Pick Up Sticks...any exciting plans you'd like to share?

Um, that information is in a hermetically sealed mayonnaise jar underneath the porch of Road to Ruin Bar in Logan New Mexico. No one knows the contents.

EMILY PEACOCK

Name: **Emily Peacock**

Company Name: **Emily Peacock**

Founded in: **2007**

Location: **Buckinghamshire, UK**

No. of Employees: **3**

Website: **www.emilypeacock.com**

Emily Peacock trained as a graphic and packaging designer and worked in a typography and typesetting studio before turning to the medium of textiles, and particularly tapestry. UK-based Emily's range of tapestry and cushion kits are instantly recognizable for their bold, fun and quirky designs, and have been featured on many TV shows, magazines and sold to crafters around the world.

Please tell us a bit about your career/background and how the Emily Peacock kit range came about?

I worked for many years in Graphic design, learning 'on the job' in design studios, typesetters and packaging design companies. Although I really enjoyed my work, I used to go home and stitch and sew—this was my real passion and I always had projects of one type or another on the go.

I think I was like a lot of people—I really felt I had something creative to give but I couldn't find exactly what it was. I used to try many different ideas and just end up frustrated. Looking back, I think my thought process was that I had to come up with something that fell in with an existing market, rather than creating something new.

I moved with my husband and children to France in 2003 and it was a tough time. We had very little income and I found it hard to settle. In short, I felt lonely and lost and began to wonder what I was made of. In the UK it was easier to be distracted by my working life, friends and family and delay finding what it was I wanted to do, but in France I felt I had no excuse and if I didn't grab the moment I would maybe feel that I had let myself down. I decided to order some wools and start playing. I experimented with different wools and canvases and decided I liked cross stitch on canvas the best. I then started to make the sort of cushions I would want in my home.

We returned to England in 2007 with very little money, no jobs to go to and just this idea of selling my cushion designs as needlepoint kits. It seemed that every door I knocked on opened and I think it's because my product was original and coincided with the revolution in craft taking place in the UK. Within no time my work was appearing in magazines and my kits were being sold in Liberty.

Describe the space you work from? How do you make it inspiring as well as functional?

Since we came back from France we have rented houses. In 4 years we have moved four times as we needed bigger and bigger properties for me to work in. In my current house I have a studio to work out of. I think there is a tendency to imagine designers wafting round in their creative space, sucking a pencil waiting for the muse to strike, but with me it's hard graft and functionality. I keep files of images that inspire me, but I mostly carry my ideas in my head.

Do you produce all of your kits yourself? How did you source all the components and find the right parts? Do you personally make each kit yourself?

I used Appleton's wools years before I started producing kits. I love their color range and the fact that they do 2 weights of wool and so that choice was obvious to me. My knowledge of needlework was quite extensive through years of teaching myself, so I knew exactly where to go for wool and canvas.

I was making all the kits myself but demand became far too high. I outsource winding wool and have it returned by the bin bag. My assistant Katie cuts the canvases and sometimes I lend a hand at putting kits together depending on how busy I am. I mainly sell direct to customers through my website and do not get involved in large orders as I simply do not have the set up. Having said that, even direct sales are becoming too much for me and for my wool supplier, so I am looking to completely change the way I operate and maybe involve a fulfillment company.

How did you work out what prices to retail your kits at? Is there a formula that you use?

I worked out my prices on store mark-up. In other words I added up all my costs (including my time), added a small realistic profit that I would be happy with if large quantities were ordered and then worked out a typical store mark-up. My kits are not cheap but they are competitively priced for this type of product

Your online store is fab! Please discuss your experiences/thoughts/tips on managing stock/shipping to customers/accepting returns etc? Do you also sell on Etsy?

Thanks! Shipping to customers and accepting returns is simple. I ship everything signed for and very little is ever returned. I am happy to accept returns up to 60 days from date of order. Stock is another matter. I have had huge issues with the dyers keeping up with my demand. I buy my wool by bags of 200 hanks and try to ensure I have plenty in stock but I have had to state on my website that colors in my designs may vary. I think of all the tasks involved in running a business, stock is the biggest headache.

Etsy is a dream. It's so simple to set up and keeps excellent records of what has been sold and which product has had the most views and so on, plus it has a huge global audience that is not easy to reach through other methods. There is a small charge for each transaction but when you bear in mind that you are effectively getting a store front where people can search for your product by name and type, it's a very inexpensive way to get started.

You now have an assistant—Katie. How did you know it was time to start employing someone rather than continue to juggle all the balls yourself? How did you know you could afford it?

Katie is in fact my sister. We have a great relationship and really see eye to eye design-wise. I needed an assistant for a while as I seemed to be constantly drowning in work and my turnover had been consistently high enough to warrant hiring help. Katie seemed the obvious choice.

Trade Fairs – An expensive, but necessary tool? Do you need to do these to get into shops?

I am not looking to increase my trade sales at the moment, so these fairs are not suitable for my business. I have done some consumer shows in London—*Stitch and Craft* at Olympia and *The Knitting & Stitching Show* at Alexander Palace—but the cost of the show versus the amount of direct sales I get is not really worth the time.

You sell directly to the public via your website AND wholesale to lots of shops and online stores. What % of your business would you say is wholesale vs retail. Is it really worth selling to shops when the margins are much lower than selling directly to your customers?

I don't wholesale my kits to lots of shops. I sell to Liberty and a couple of small shops but I have had to draw the line as demand was too high. I sell 98% of my kits through my website and Etsy and the other 2% through other outlets. As long as I have to be in charge of production, I will not be increasing my trade sales. I feel I have an original idea and I am not willing to work late into the night for very small profit to fulfill trade orders. If my production methods change then I will happily do as much wholesale as I can.

Cashflow/finances—one of the biggest challenges of a small business owner. How have you financed the growth of your company—did you have to approach the banks for loans? How do you make sure retailers pay you on time?

I have never had a loan or borrowed money for my business. I started small and paid for what I could afford and always invested profits into stock. My circle of stockists is very small, I have a good working relationship with all of them and I have never had a problem with payment.

You don't get rich by having a book out and my decision to do a book came
from the same place as my decision to start a business—it was simply something
I wanted to do. I can honestly say that money has never been a factor in any
decision I have ever made. If you have an idea it has to come from a place of
personal passion, belief and integrity, definitely not from 'what would make
me rich?'

I have been approached by a few publishers. My book was published by GMC and
their offer came at a time when I was working with my friend Jessica Aldred from
The Royal School of Needlework. We were discussing doing 'something' together,
so we decided to write a good technical book. You are paid a small advance whilst
you compile the book and then you receive royalties based on sales. The book is
a collaboration and so there are elements of me and elements of Jessica in it.
What is extremely challenging is the deadlines you are given. We produced the
book in 9 months which was quite a feat given the amount of work involved and
I could not have possibly done it alone. If I were to do a book again I would take
my time, probably just stick to cross stitch and canvas work and only approach
a publisher once I had sufficient material.

Your kits designs have such a unique and individual look. Have your designs
or ideas ever been copied/ripped off? What happened? What did you do?
Discuss...

When I began my business my methods were unique—there was no one using
2 counts of canvas and 2 types of wool in counted cross stitch. The needlepoint kit
designs available tended to be traditional and I believe I was the first to introduce
lettering adopted from my years in Graphic Design, along with my bright color
palette. I have had my methods directly copied and my modern design ideas
adopted. It never feels good to have this happen to you. You have arrived at the
place you are in through your own thoughts and you have taken risks and gone
through finding the strength and confidence to be there, so when someone takes
these ideas from you it is not only immoral, it feels like a very personal theft.

I delight in designers contributing their own modern take on needlepoint and this is
by no means a turf war, but directly copying methods and ideas is shameless and
not to be tolerated. That sounds strong, but protecting original thought is something
I feel very strongly about and I make no apologies for being vocal about it. If you
like the way someone thinks, commission them.

You can protect your designs through organizations such as ACID, but there are
many situations where there is not much you can do apart from confront. Of course

thieves tend to also be liars and will deny any wrong doing, so the best thing you can do is to put your efforts into producing good, original work.

What do you wish you'd know back when you started out?

The biggest mistake I have ever made was to say yes to too many things. I think there's a tendency when you begin a business to be so flattered by any attention you get and so worried that it could all dry up tomorrow, that you say yes to everything. I see things differently now and I try to put myself first, protect myself and put my energy in the right places. In the past I have been in a position where I have had to force designs out whilst dealing with huge quantities of orders and that never works and I end up feeling depleted and that I've let myself down.

The other thing I would say is to trust your own instincts. If you really believe you have something to offer, then go with it. I have been told by many well-meaning individuals what I should be designing and how I should be running my business and I have nodded politely then gone and done exactly what feels right for me. You will be offered all sorts of well meaning advice, but nobody can think for you and no one else is living your life. You have to be single-minded and not swayed by fear and opinion.

And finally...what does the future hold for Emily Peacock...any exciting plans you'd like to share?

That's a hard one, it reminds me of the expression "if you want to make God laugh, tell him your plans." I couldn't have envisaged the path I've been down—all the great experiences I've had and the wonderful people I've met. I will always be a needlework devotee, but would like to explore it in different forms. I would like more design time so I am working towards moving production to a place that takes the pressure off me and can fulfill trade orders. I have also started running workshops and these have been so enjoyable and I have had such great feedback that I really want to do more of these. The main thing is to make decisions that keep needlework moving forward and make people inspired enough to give it a try.

crow and canary
fine art card + gift representation

Name: **Carina Murray**

Company Name: **Crow and Canary**

Founded in: **2006**

Location: **Portland, Oregon**

No. of Reps: **4**

Website: **www.crowandcanary.com**

Crow and Canary is a travel-based repping agency, specializing in Fine Art, Card & Gift Representation, covering territories including Oregon, Washington, California, New York, New Jersey and Connecticut. A focus on handmade products, eco-friendly practices and a talented line up of local and national designers, are just a few of the qualities that set Crow and Canary apart in the industry

Founded by Carina Murray in 2006, the company has gone on to represent a diverse line up of designers – though letterpress, screen-printed and hand embellished cards remain at the core of the collection. Carina is a true champion of independent stationers and hopes that her passion and adoration for her job comes through via her blog and many social media endeavors. You can most often find Carina with her trusty canine companion, Ula, en route to show eager shops the latest and greatest from the C&C collection!

You represent a great selection of greetings card and stationery companies— so, what exactly does a "Rep" do then?

Reps are essentially a liaison between the designer and wholesale buyer. We show samples to buyers and forward the orders on to the lines we represent. We are not responsible for production or shipping. Our job is strictly commission-based, 10-25% is the industry norm. Most reps only take commission on orders paid, meaning if a retailer cancels the order or does not follow through with payment, the rep doesn't receive commission.

I work primarily as a traveling rep. I visit stores in the Pacific NW and have three additional sub-reps that call on their own territories. We work much in the fashion of an old-school traveling salesman. We also exhibit at several trade shows a year, including the New York International Gift Fair and the National Stationery Show. Participation in trade shows is optional and requires a participation fee, along with standard commission. This is an excellent option for most designers, as exhibiting at a trade show as a single entity is a rather large undertaking and expense.

Tell us a bit about your background—what were you doing before founding Crow and Canary, and when/where did the idea for the business come from?

My degree is in fine art photography; I interned at a photography gallery in Seattle, Washington during college and went on to work as the assistant director after graduating. I also have a background in the optical world, having worked on and off as an Optician for many years, that was my fallback trade before I launched my company. Having primarily worked for small business owners, I have had some excellent mentors to learn from and many of the bits of wisdom that I've picked up translate to any industry.

In 2006 I'd become a bit burned out at my 9-5 job. I had recently met a designer with a successful card company and began helping her with production and fulfillment on the side. She planted the seed that working as a manufacturer's representative could be a low overhead and flexible business idea and she happened to be looking for a rep on the West Coast. I was quite excited about the thought, as I've always been a stationery fanatic and during college spent some time printmaking and setting type for letterpress. I quit my day job in September of 2006 and Crow and Canary was officially born!

Describe the early days of your business? How did you make ends meet? Do you remember your first sale/order? How long did it take before you were making enough to live on?

Business was slow going at first. I started representing just one line; I now work with 28 manufacturers. I was fortunate that both retailers and designers were willing to take a chance on me.

I distinctly remember the initial nervousness of cold-calling stores and stopping in to introduce myself. My first order was with a well-known Los Angeles paper boutique and they continue to be a loyal account. I'm forever grateful that they were welcoming to me and helped build my confidence to keep reaching out to retailers.

I would estimate that it took over 12 months before I was able to support myself through the business. I was fortunate to have a savings account to dip into and my husband was able to provide us health insurance benefits through his employer.

What do you look for when taking on a new brand?

I'm rather specific in what I look for when I consider adding a new line to my repertoire. Here are a few of my considerations:

The line must be complementary to my current collection; if it's too similar to designs I already represent, I risk competition within my own collection.

I'm always on the lookout for innovative products. If I see a line and think: "Wow, that's so unique"—it's definitely a contender.

Good product photography, a comprehensive website and catalog and flexibility are key.

I find it easier to rep lines that have at least 40 unique designs, though this is not a hard and fast rule.

Lines that work with eco-friendly goods are also a plus.

Would you ever Rep a designer/brand who had literally just designed their first range and hadn't yet sold into stores themselves? Or do you prefer them to have established a track record in their area first?

I believe it's vital that designers do as much for their brand themselves as they can initially. There is a refinement process that happens for most new lines and it's invaluable to receive direct feedback about pricing, designs, paper quality, etc. I typically tell designers to "wear as many hats" within their company as they can, for as long as they can. There will come a point when tasks, including sales, need to be delegated and that is usually when working with a rep is the next natural step.

I rarely approach brand new manufacturers. I do think a good track record is important and I take a lot of feedback under consideration from the shop owners and buyers that I work with. If I consistently hear that a line is selling well and that the designer is easy to work with, I'm more likely to approach that line if it fits my aesthetic.

At what stage in the business did you take on your first employee—was it a big leap from doing everything yourself to hiring others? How did you know you were ready and the business could afford it?

I had toyed with the idea of hiring a sub-rep for several years, but never seriously pursued it. I'd gone as far as including a blurb on my website that said I was seeking a sub-rep in the San Francisco/Bay Area. I'd occasionally receive an inquiry from someone, mostly folks without any background in the stationery industry. In April of 2010, Kendra Gjerseth contacted me—she couldn't have been a better match! Kendra had been a paper boutique owner and manufacturer in the stationery world and was looking to start a career in the repping world. It was really an easy and natural transition, I didn't have much to lose as I was simply paying her for orders that she generated and providing her with some sales materials and tools. Having Kendra onboard really changed the way I viewed my business, I've since gone on to hire two additional reps in other territories and I am open to the idea of expanding into more areas if I were to find the right people.

The greetings card market is so competitive these days? Any advice for new young designers about to take the leap?

Definitely attend the *National Stationery Show* and/or a major wholesale gift show near you and see what you're up against. It's really important to walk the show floor and see what other people are selling. Perhaps your million-dollar idea was just launched by another company. Know who your competitors are and figure out the edge that you offer that sets your brand apart.

Take part in social networking; I was a naysayer myself—I won't lie. Twitter alone has completely revolutionized my business. I've been able to develop relationships with buyers, designers and press that would not have otherwise been accessible to me. Be a part of industry conversations. Establish yourself as a knowledgeable go-to person. Positive, tangible benefits will follow, I promise!

I love creative and unique greetings, but don't forget to focus on occasions that sell. You can never have too many birthday cards, with thank you and love coming in as a close second. Listen to what buyers need; if you're working with a store that says they can't find enough good sympathy cards create a design to fill that need if it fits within your brand.

How should new designers go about finding the right Rep for them?

An online presence of independent sales reps and repping agencies is surprisingly low. These are some of the routes I know of:

- *The National Stationery Show* typically has a listing in the lobby of the convention center for 'Rep's seeking Lines' and vice-versa. If you are exhibiting at a wholesale show, place a "reps wanted" sign in your booth.

- Most gift show and wholesale tradeshow websites list the names of reps exhibiting in current or past shows. You may consider checking out a local wholesale gift show to introduce yourself to some reps. It's usually not too hard to gain a free day pass if you're able to show your business credentials to the show manager.

- Ask some of the retailers you work with. I frequently get inquiries from designers that have gotten my name from buyers I do business with.

- Ask other designers you're friendly with, not everyone is willing to share this sort of information, but it never hurts to ask.

- Lastly, get creative with your google searches. 'Manufacturer's Representative' is only a jumping off point in terms of keywords.

Once you sign up with a rep for a certain region, do you have to pay them commission for any and all shops you have product in within that region? What if you already had shops in place before you signed on with them? What if shops approach you directly without having ever interacted with the rep?

This will definitely vary by rep. I personally write individual contracts for new lines and am usually willing to negotiate, regarding existing accounts. One thing to consider—designers typically receive re-orders more steadily when working with reps, as reps tend to see stores on a quarterly basis. Although you'd be out the commission, you'd likely be ahead in the long run. There are some stores that prefer to order directly from the designer. Because these are few and far between, most of the lines I work with still pay commission on these orders. If you are considering working with a rep, I'd recommend that you get answers to these questions directly and be sure to draw up a contract that restates all of the information you and the rep agreed to verbally.

Any tips for approaching buyers and getting my line into stores myself?

I would encourage any line looking for more exposure to send press kits to magazines, as well as emails to design blogs. In terms of contacting out-of-town stores, my method is to first call and politely request the name of the buyer. I typically mention that it's for the purpose of sending catalogs and rarely have anyone decline to give me the contact name. From there, I would go all out in creating a package for your catalog that's enticing to open. You may consider using themes from your line. Brand cohesiveness and a bit of ingenuity go a long way! Your mailing will be memorable and stand out among the many submissions stores receive. Be sure to follow-up by phone or email. Tenacity is key! In a perfect world, you wouldn't have to follow-up with stores, they'd see the product and order it that instant. However, I find that most buyers have so much going on that they don't mind a few reminder emails or calls. Unless a buyer explicitly says they aren't interested, I continue to stay in contact with them.

Because greetings cards are relatively low value items, what sort of wholesale minimums would you suggest?

$100 is the average minimum order and I find that most stores don't have a problem reaching minimums. It's perfectly appropriate to have a minimum on paper, but be willing to be flexible with stores if they request a reduced minimum. If your cards sell well they will surely order above the minimum next time. It's really about building lasting relationships with retailers, so be willing to break your own rules sometimes.

Most cards are sold in 6's and occasionally dozens. Most of the stores I work with prefer to buy in 6's, as that allows them a larger selection of designs. Gift items and items with higher price points are often sold in 3's or 4's.

Because of the fairly low price points/profit margins of greetings cards, you would need to sell pretty high volume every month to earn a decent living. I guess those sort of production numbers are achievable when using a commercial printer, but is it hard for designers to produce, and earn a living from, hand-made /hand-printed cards?

The advantage of printing your own goods is that you don't have to stock a large inventory, which can be challenging to find space for and it's often hard to predict which styles will sell well. The initial investment is also lower, since you can print to order if necessary, whereas commercial printers require high minimums per piece in order to get a price break. It's also easy to prototype designs and wait for feedback. If a style is not well received it can be scrapped without much loss.

The disadvantage of printing your own goods is that the production time can be a bit long and tedious and if it becomes necessary to hire production help, this can also begin to gobble up profit margins. I have seen a handful of companies that have gone under from not being able to keep up with the success and production demands as they grow. I think a good business plan and a reliable team can help circumvent that sort of demise.

When should new holiday card ranges be released?

It's imperative to time your seasonal releases with the industry standards. This really is a case of "the early bird gets the worm"! Buyers begin writing holiday orders (Halloween, Christmas, Hanukkah) as early as May and June. It's really easy to miss out on a large chunk of sales if your new designs aren't ready to show. Another big seasonal release is Valentine's Day. I start showing Valentine's as early as October. Most buyers don't see reps between Thanksgiving and Christmas, so it's definitely helpful to have these out early. For spring occasions (Easter, Mother's Day, Father's Day and Graduation) I would recommend a release date in early January.

What does the future hold for Crow and Canary...any exciting plans you'd like to share?

Having just brought on a full-time rep in Los Angeles and the New York tri-state area 7 months ago, I'm really focusing my energy on helping grow those territories. For the first time, Crow & Canary will have booths at the winter and summer *New York International Gift Fair* and *The National Stationery Show* this year. This is a big and exciting undertaking for us and we know will lead to some new opportunities. I've also been expanding my consulting offerings for manufacturers that are new to the industry.

Craft Business Heroes:
30 Creative Entrepreneurs
Share the Secrets Of Their Success

If you've enjoyed reading the stories from other Crafty Entrepreneurs featured in this book—are you ready for more?

Amy Butler, Subversive Cross Stitch's Julie Jackson, Amy Karol, Poppy Treffry, Sublime Stitching's Jenny Hart, Jeweler of the Year Alex Monroe and lots more successful creative business owners share the stories of how they built their business and achieved craft business success. Prepare to be inspired!

Search under: Craft Business Heroes / ISBN: 978-1-908707-02-4

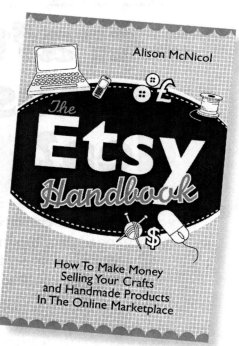

Do you have a craft business idea?

Would you like to sell the products you make? Start with a great logo, business cards and a website and you could soon be turning your creative dreams into reality!

Approaching a designer doesn't have to be scary or expensive and can really help get your new business up and running. Seeing your scribbled ideas transform into finished graphics is often the first time you really start to feel like a 'business' and with ongoing support and advice, the great little design company can help your new business fly.

Logos • Stationery • Websites • Flyers • Brochures • Adverts Banners • Packaging • Labels • Book design • Illustration

For all enquiries please email
julie@thegreatlittledesigncompany.com
www.thegreatlittledesigncompany.com

Resources

Business Help

USA

SCORE (Service Corps of Retired Executives): www.score.org

SBDC (Small Business Development Center): www.sba.gov

UK

Business Link: www.businesslink.gov.uk

Domain Names

www.godaddy.com   www.godaddy.com/uk

www.register.com   www.namesecure.com

www.ukwebsolutionsdirect.co.uk

Company Names Registers and Trademarks

www.secstates.com   www.copyright.gov

www.uspto.gov   www.companieshouse.gov.uk

www.ipo.gov.uk

Business Plan Templates

USA

SCORE (Service Corps of Retired Executives):
www.score.org/template_gallery.html

SBA (Small Business Administration):
www.sba.gov/starting_business/planning/writingplan.html

WBDC (Women's Business Development Center):
http://www2.wbdc.org/tools/develop/develop.asp

UK

Business Link: www.businesslink.org.uk

Finding Vendors

Thomasnet.com   Alibaba.com

Finding A Sales Rep

UAMR: http://www.uamr.com

RepHunter: http://www.rephunter.net/

GreatRep: http://www.greatrep.com/

Manufacturer's Representatives Wanted:
http://www.manufacturers-representatives.com/

Manufacturer's Representative Profile: http://www.mrpusa.com/

Sales Agent USA: http://www.salesagentusa.com/

www.findfashionrep.com

Online Store Building Sites

www.shopify.com   www.bigcartel.com   www.bigcommerce.com

www.ekmpowershop.com   www.moonfruit.com   www.volusion.com

Blog Building Tools

www.wordpress.org   www.typepad.com   www.blogger.com

Trade Shows

New York International Gift Fair: www.nyigf.com

Craft & Hobby Association: www.chashow.com

Philadelphia Buyers Marker on American Craft:
www.buyersmarketofamericancraft.com

Dallas Market Center: www.dallasmarketcenter.com

California Market Center: www.californiamarketcenter.com

Chicago Merchandise Mart: www.merchandisemart.com

International Gem & Jewelry: www.intergem.com (Trade & consumer)

Craft Shows

USA

Bazaar Bizarre: www.bazaarbizarre.org

Maker Faire: www.makerfaire.com

Renegade Craft Fairs: www.renegadecraft.com

American Craft Council Show: www.public.craftcouncil.org/baltimore

UK

ICHF: www.ichf.co.uk

Twisted Thread: www.twistedthread.com

Aztec Events: www.aztecevents.co.uk

Online Marketplaces

www.etsy.com   www.bonanza.com   www.folksy.com

www.madeit.com.au   www.notonthehighstreet.com   www.ebay.com

Other Resources

Adjust images: www.shrinkpictures.com

Cool Business Cards: www.moo.com

Lightning Source UK Ltd.
Milton Keynes UK
UKOW051304190313

207868UK00012B/186/P